SISTER WENDY'S
BOOK OF
SAINTS

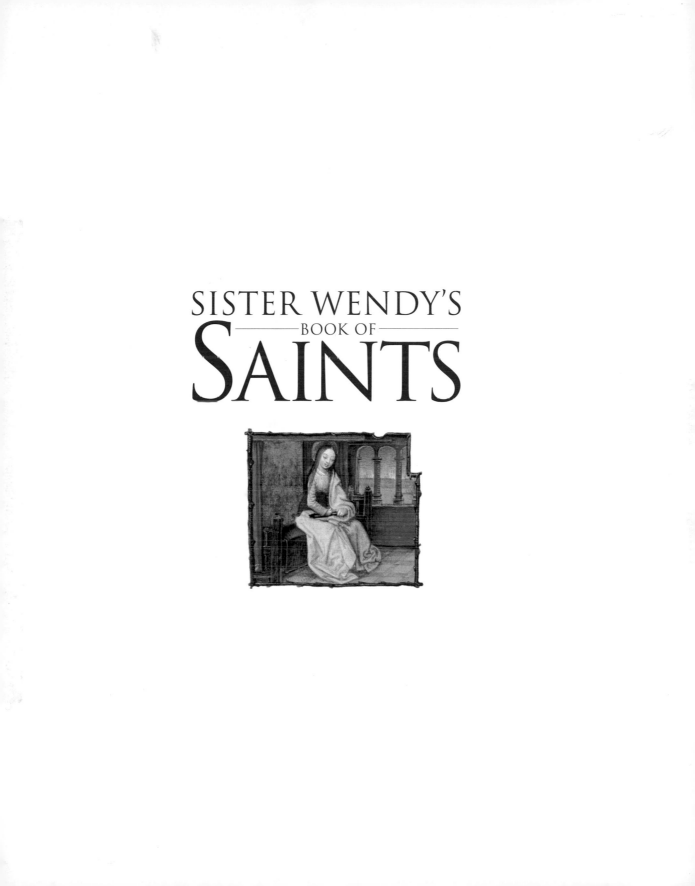

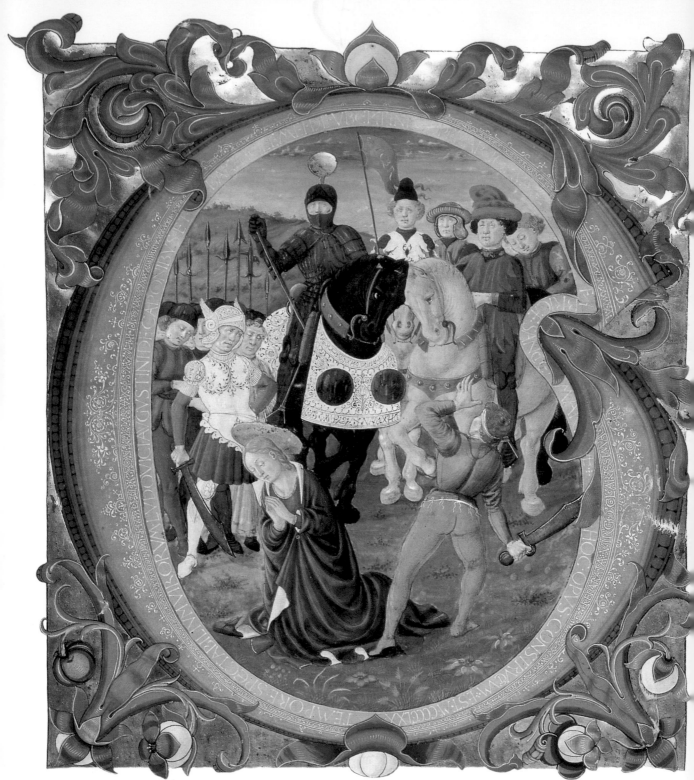

THE MARTYRDOM OF SAINT REPARATA
Little is known of the life and death of St. Reparata, the subject of
this beautiful and intriguing image. Popular in Europe during
medieval times, her feast day is celebrated on October 8th.

SISTER WENDY'S
BOOK OF
SAINTS

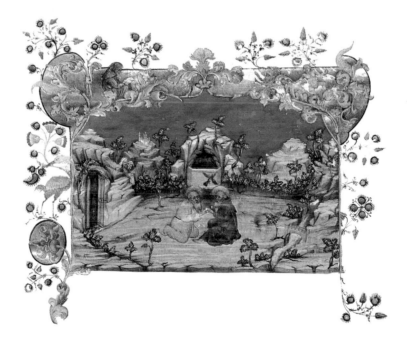

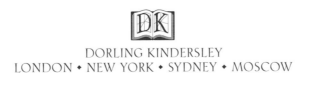

DORLING KINDERSLEY
LONDON • NEW YORK • SYDNEY • MOSCOW

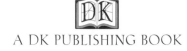

A DK PUBLISHING BOOK

In conjunction with
ROSE Publishing Limited

Project Editor
Colette Connolly

Designers
Joanne Long • Claire Naylor

Editors
Lara Maiklem • Jo Marceau

Design Assistant
Richard Sinclair

Senior Editor
Luci Collings

Senior Art Editor
Claire Legemah

Production
Meryl Silbert

Deputy Art Director
Tina Vaughan

US Editor
Mary Sutherland

AUTHOR'S DEDICATION

*For my sister Pamela Paton, who will greet with literate hilarity
the idea that she might be within sighting distance of sanctity*

2 4 6 8 10 9 7 5 3

Library of Congress Cataloging-in-Publication Data

Beckett, Wendy.

Sister Wendy's book of saints / Wendy Beckett. -- 1st American ed.
p. cm.
ISBN 0-7894-2398-7
1. Christian saints--Biography. I. Biblioteca apostolica vaticana. II. Title.
BX4655.2.B44 1998
270'.0922--dc21
[B]

97-33492
CIP

Visit us on the World Wide Web at http://www.dk.com

Reproduced in Italy by GRB.
Printed and bound in Italy.

CONTENTS

ILLUMINATED SAINTS

ILLUMINATED manuscripts come in all sizes: from very small, to fit into a wealthy purse, to very large, to stand on a lectern in a monastic church. When they are adorned with miniatures of the saints there is the same variety, from tiny figures within initials to paintings that the whole congregation can see.

Small or great, the paintings have but one purpose: they are there to help toward prayer. The saints are the people, weak and imperfect like ourselves, who said a total "Yes" to God's love. It is not that they were strong enough or virtuous enough to win his love, because that love is always freely given, but only those we call saints actually did that blessed taking, accepted the reality of being

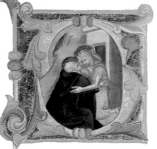

ST. ANTHONY AND ST. PAUL

loved with all its consequences. Since God's definition is simply "love," the saint surrenders to its meaning.

This tiny picture (*see also p.67*) shows love at its simplest. The aged St. Anthony Abbot, living alone in the desert, is embracing the still more aged St. Paul, the first hermit. The two saints, who spent their days lost in prayer, who have no visitors and never speak, are both responding to this encounter with warm affection. They do not stand back and assess each other; they make no judgements. A stranger has appeared, and they open wide their arms. To accept people as they are, without fretting at what they are not or wanting to change them, is the essence of love. It gives; it seeks the good of the other and not its own. As an earlier St. Paul, the apostle, said, love is "always ready to excuse, to trust, to hope, and to endure."

But love is complex, in that it can be selfish to excuse and to trust, always to say "Yes," when the doing so is not to the other's real good. Christ himself had no hesitation in saying "No," as when the mother of the two apostles James and John asked for a special place of honor for her sons. It would not have been to their good. Christ, of course, could see this, because he is wisdom incarnate, and unless we share in this holy wisdom, we can be shamefully weak in what we call "love." In the Bible,

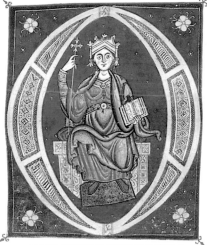

SOPHIA, PERSONIFICATION OF WISDOM

wisdom is seen as a woman — Sophia in the Greek, Sapienta in the Latin. The author of the Old Testament Book of Wisdom speaks of her with awe: "She is a breath of the power of God . . . a reflection of the eternal light." But he also speaks with emotion: "I loved her more than health and beauty . . . she is an inexhaustible treasure to men . . . I resolved to have her as my bride, I feel in love with her beauty." It is wisdom that makes love practical, not just pleasing in the head. We need this virtue to control us, and that is how this artist portrays her — as a queen. She seems to float in a starry sky, enthroned, holding aloft, in one slender elegant hand, the scepter of the cross (that wisdom which is foolishness to men), and in the other, holding out for us to read, the scriptures. She is crowned and adorned, a figure clad in the rich amplitude of royalty, solemn but not severe, making demands upon us but only that we might be where she is, in the light of God. There is no saint who does not long for wisdom, and she is always there in answer to our prayer.

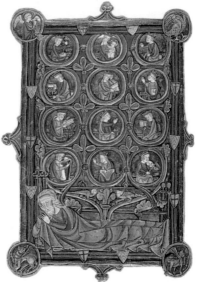

THE TREE OF JESSE

Holiness can so easily appear as something remote from us, to be read about or, as in these illuminated manuscripts, to be gazed at, but from afar. Yet to be a saint is a wholly practical and realistic growth into our own truth. It is what we are all meant to become, it is our deepest fulfillment, our own personal realization of what we have been potentially from birth. There is no play about sanctity. It starts from where we are and what we are. The Tree of Jesse shows the ancestry of Christ, or at least part of it. Jesse was the father of King David, seen here as a musician because he wrote the psalms; David's son was King Solomon, the architect of the Temple, and so on right up to the Virgin Mary with Jesus in her arms. The ancestors of Christ are a mixed bunch, since David committed murder and Solomon had numerous wives, but these were the genes he inherited and which he accepted as his humanity. Sanctity means recognizing the whole of us, the generic flaws that God's grace must purify and the genetic virtues that grace must also infuse, in case we rely on their natural power. There is no part of us that we must sweep under a mental carpet, determined to show God only the nice parts. He knows, far better than we ever shall, what we are really like, and how much of it is our "fault." Jesus did not choose his family tree any more than we do. We and he were born with it, and this unique "us," with such-and-such an ancestor, is the person God knows and loves. At the corners of the great Tree of Jesse stand the symbols of the four evangelists, who wrote the Gospels that teach us about Christ, who came that we "might have life, life to the full," and to receive that life we must be completely there, true to what we are.

A saint is loving, wise, which means he or she has common sense to a sublime degree, is genuine, and a person of integrity. Is that it? Not quite, because all these gifts have to be directed, harnessed, and centered, and the center is Jesus Christ. St. Paul speaks of having "the mind of Christ" and that for him, "to live is Christ." The pictures of the saints show us men and women for whom what their brother Paul said is true. They read the Gospels, which tell us about Christ, they spent their time in prayer, which allows the spirit of Jesus to utter within us his absolute Amen to whatever the Father wills. It is spelled out for us in silver and gold and precious stones on this glorious book cover. There, in the center, is the slight but majestic figure of the Lord, his hand raised in gentle blessing. Above him is the angel Gabriel, who announced his coming, and below him the prophet Elijah, who foretold it. All around are the apostles and evangelists, those who knew Jesus and shared their transforming knowledge with us in the New Testament. Some look young and some look old; basically it is much the same face, give or take a beard or two. It is not these men as personalities that interest the artist here, but these men as examples. They are nothing in themselves, it is the centrality of Jesus that gives them meaning. To be centered is the most important choice we can ever make, and the grace of God waits patiently for our acceptance. We are inadequate: the one full human, as the artist depicts him, is Jesus, there for us to love, to learn by, to be made true by.

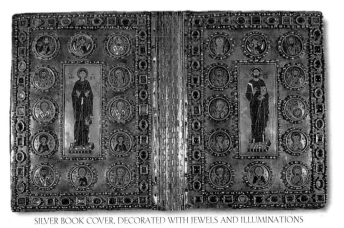

SILVER BOOK COVER, DECORATED WITH JEWELS AND ILLUMINATIONS

ST PETER

Leader of the apostles and first pope

died c.64

FEAST DAY
June 29th

PATRON SAINT
*Rome, fishermen,
longevity*

ATTRIBUTES
keys, cockerel

WHEN JESUS CHOSE his twelve apostles he appointed Peter to lead them. Jesus made a pun about his name; he said, "you are Peter [which in Latin means rock] and on this rock I will build my church," but nobody was ever less like rock than this warm-hearted and incorrigibly impulsive man. St. Peter is so appealing because he has all our foolishness; if only we had some of his faith. This is illustrated by the wonderful story of Peter walking on the water. There was a great storm — here you can see the masts actually being snapped on the apostles' boat — and when the storm was at its height Jesus walked across the water and summoned Peter. It is at this point that we witness Peter's faith, for he obeys, jumps in, and starts walking on the water. Then we see his foolishness — just like us — he suddenly realizes "what am I doing?" and he sinks. Here we see Jesus pulling Peter out of the water, and saying to him, "O man of little faith, why did you doubt?"

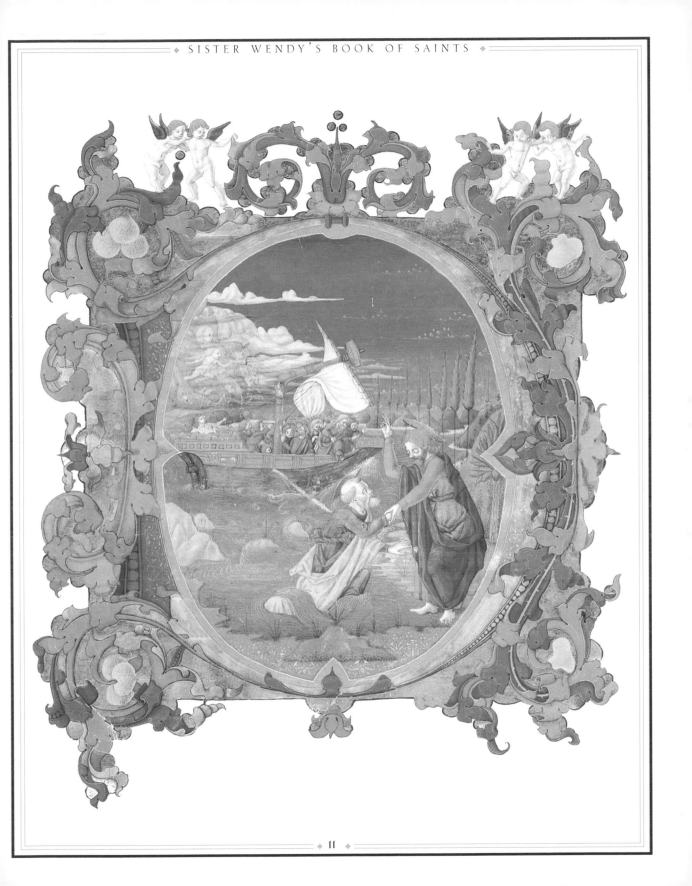

ST. PETER
Leader of the apostles and first pope

died c.64

FEAST DAY
June 29th

PATRON SAINT
*Rome, fishermen,
longevity*

ATTRIBUTES
keys, cockerel

ONE OF THE NICEST THINGS about St. Peter was that he never thought he was special. So when, toward the end of his life in Rome (when he was being savagely persecuted), he was thrown into prison, he sat there patiently, waiting for the end. Then the miracle happens.

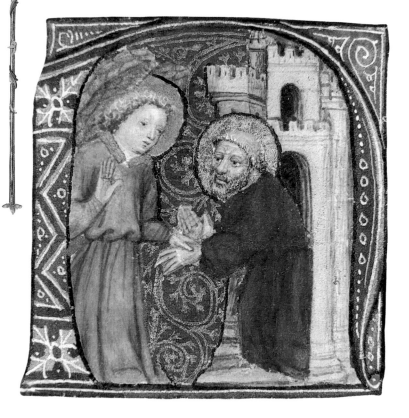

One night, he went to sleep and dreamed that his whole prison was filled with light, and an angel came and took him by the hand. Here you can see it happening. With the greatest tenderness, a glorious pink and golden angel is leading Peter out of his prison, leaving the little castle behind. It has a dreamlike feel. They get to doors that open miraculously; they pass people who simply do not see them; Peter is convinced he is sleeping. The angel takes him right into the city, and then leaves him. It is only when Peter opens his eyes that he realizes it was not a dream at all, God has rescued him. He has escaped because there is still something else he has to do: he has to be ready, finally, to die on the cross for Christ.

ST THOMAS
The apostle of India

died 53

FEAST DAY
December 21st

PATRON SAINT
Prato, Parma, Urbino, judges, builders, architects, theologians

ATTRIBUTES
spear, belt, or girdle of the Virgin Mary

ST THOMAS IS A SAINT with whom we all identify, because here was one of Jesus' twelve chosen apostles, and he doubted. You remember the story: Jesus has risen from the dead and he appears to the apostles, and Thomas is not there. When Thomas does turn up he finds them in a state of excitement, overcome with joy. Thomas is completely unconvinced. We can imagine him saying to himself, "This is some kind of group hysteria, their grief has made them imagine this." The more they insist that Jesus has really appeared to them, the more Thomas denies it: "Until I actually see him and put my fingers into those wounds, I will not believe it is the real Jesus that we saw hanging on a cross, bleeding." A week later Jesus comes and this time Thomas is there. Jesus looks at him and says "Ah, Thomas! Come and put your fingers in my wounds." Thomas is filled with shame and awe, and he sinks to his knees, saying "My Lord and my God" — one of the very rare times Jesus is called God. But Thomas has seen that dead body, and he now knows that Jesus has risen. This wonderful picture shows that happening: Thomas with a look of incredulity, modulating into conviction, and Jesus looking down with an

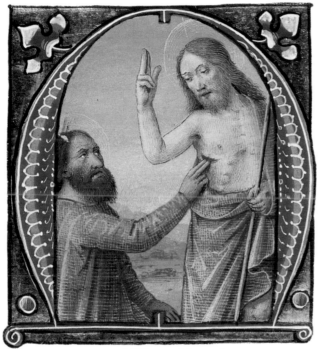

air of loving rebuke because he says to Thomas, "You only believe, Thomas, because you have seen. Blessed are those who have not seen and yet believe." And of course the reference is to us — we who have not seen and yet believe, because faith cannot depend upon proof. We need logical arguments to prove our faith is not nonsense, but if nothing contradicts itself, and this is the word of God, then we make that great leap of faith and we say "I believe, my Lord and my God." Thomas could not do that without proof, and yet he still became a saint.

ST MARK
Evangelist

died c.74

FEAST DAY
April 25th

PATRON SAINT
Venice, glaziers

ATTRIBUTES
winged lion, gospel

THE EVANGELIST ST. MARK had as his attribute a beast, the winged lion. Whoever painted this enchanting miniature had a delightful sense of humor because the lion resembles an imbecilic sheep gazing in wonderment as St. Mark sharpens his quill pen. **T**his is a highly energetic St. Mark, and legend credits him with a highly energetic career that ended in martyrdom. This is a Mark of passion and determination, so intent upon writing his gospel that he hardly needs or notices the wistful presence of the attendant lion. St. Mark's gospel concerns itself more with the Passion of Jesus than the other three, and so it is significant that his knife and the pen make a cross.

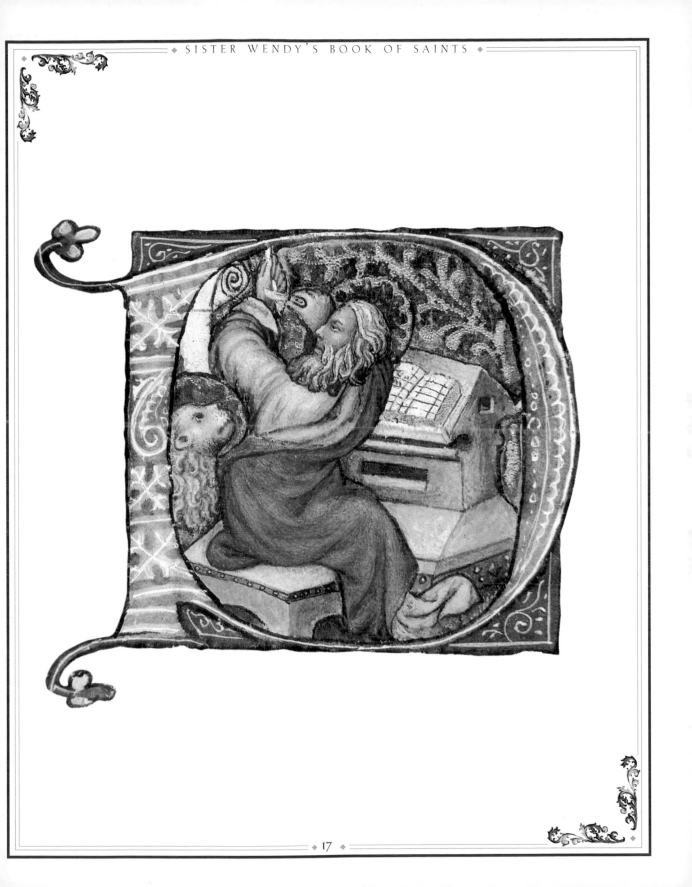

ST MARK

Evangelist

died c.74

FEAST DAY
April 25th

PATRON SAINT
Venice, glaziers

ATTRIBUTES
*winged lion,
gospel*

LEGEND SAYS ST. MARK sailed to Alexandria to become their bishop, and that the Egyptians, in their wickedness (there is little tolerance or ecumenism in medieval manuscripts), captured him while he was saying Mass. This picture represents St. Mark expressing the resigned astonishment appropriate to a saint. But his martyrdom was not the end of the story. The Venetians needed a saint to be their patron, and the controlled power of a winged lion was particularly seductive.

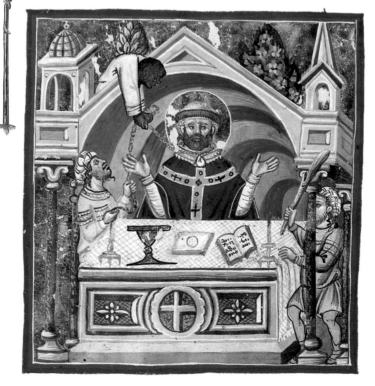

T his artist shows them stealing St. Mark's body from Alexandria and then, with great skill and duplicity, bundling it into a cask and overlaying it with the carcasses of swine, unclean meat for the devout Muslim. The swine do, in fact, look like miniature hippopotamuses, but for those who know the story, this presents no difficulties. Despite these rather disreputable

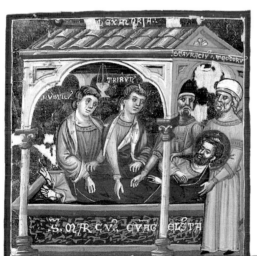

shenanigans, the Venetians truly honored St. Mark, and his winged lion became for them an inspired model of spirituality (the wings) and power (the lion). Power is always dangerous, and let us hope they prayed that winged power would have an element of purity.

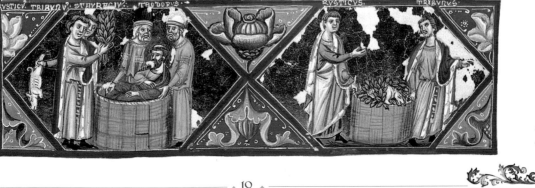

ST MATTHEW
Evangelist

1st Century

FEAST DAY
September 21st

PATRON SAINT
*accountants,
bookkeepers,
tax-collectors,
custom officers,
security guards*

ATTRIBUTES
*gospel,
money box,
glasses*

THIS IS A SPLENDID and elaborate image of St. Matthew. According to the Gospels he was the tax collector who gave up everything to follow Jesus, and one might imagine that the elaborate desk and the grand curtains and architectural details are reminiscent of his well-paid earlier career. This is, in fact, not so. This particular artist paints like this, but it seems uncannily apt. St. Matthew's symbol was the winged man because he starts his gospel with the genealogy of Christ. Of all the evangelists he was the most conscious of the humanity of Jesus, and most of the details of the Christmas story came to us from St. Matthew. There is no winged man in this picture, but there is an extraordinary vignette of the stable and the crib. It is almost as though we are being shown what is in St. Matthew's mind as he starts to write — he is going to tell us about St. Joseph and the shepherds, and the baby in a manger. The artist could have put over Matthew's head the word "thinks," as in comic books, and this vision is his inspired thought. This thought dominates him, he lives in the happiness of the birth of Christ and of all the good news (which is what "gospel" means) that this birth is, and will be, for humanity.

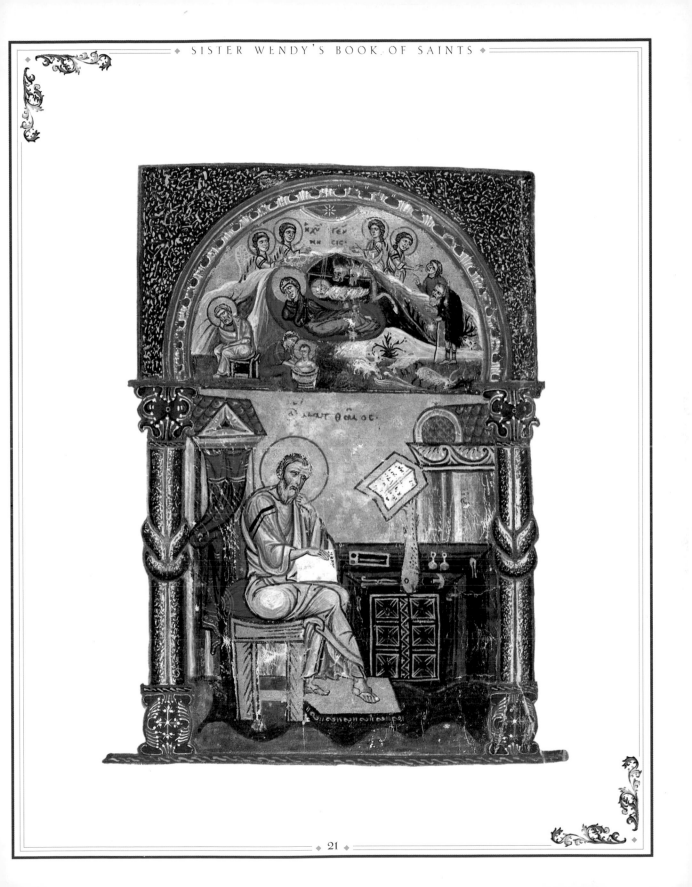

ST JOHN *the* APOSTLE
Evangelist

died c.100

FEAST DAY
December 27th

PATRON SAINT
*theologians,
writers*

ATTRIBUTES
eagle, book

ST JOHN IS SAID TO BE the only apostle who did not die a martyr's death. He lived on a long time, ending his life at Ephesus. Here he is in old age. His emblematic eagle is not physically present, but what is present is the daring flight of imagination which that eagle symbolized: the divine freedom. Old and weary, St. John is pondering on mystery of the Resurrection. We are shown his thoughts, dwelling on Christ the risen hero overcoming death, seizing by the hand the long-dead Adam and Eve, and wresting them from the grip of death into eternal life. Kings and prophets wait hopefully for the same resurrection, and so, we feel, does John himself. He is near death, but in Jesus there is only eternal life. The story goes that the old saint would be asked every Sunday to give the homily at Mass, but all he would ever say was, "Little children, love one another." When it was suggested he might vary his message, St. John seemed surprised, explaining gently that mutual love was the Lord's command, and that, if we keep it, is all we need. This frail, venerable figure reminds us, as it must have done those Ephesian congregations, that the saints do not need to "speak" to us; their very presence tells us something about God. St. John Vianney, a nineteenth-century follower of this

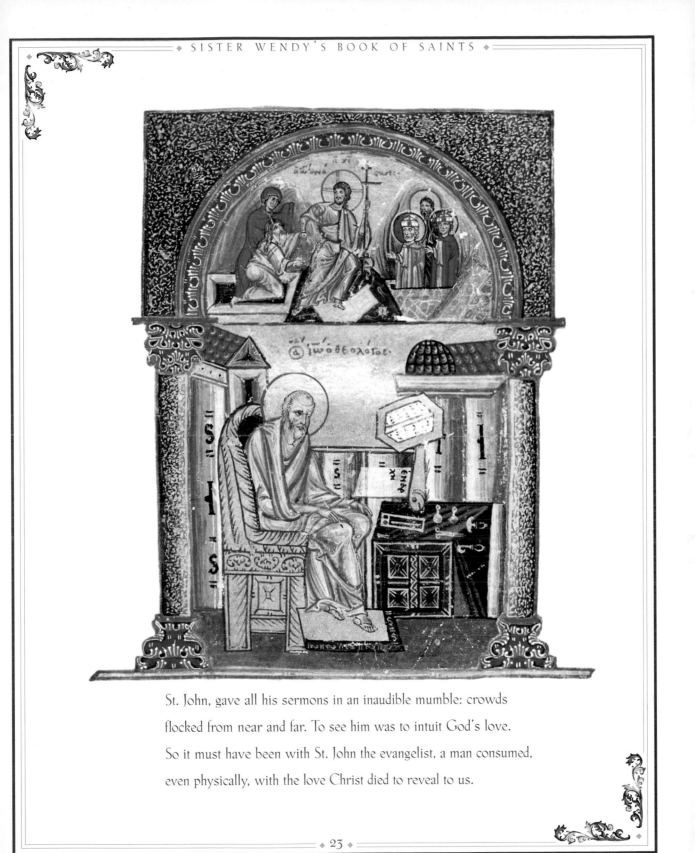

St. John, gave all his sermons in an inaudible mumble: crowds
flocked from near and far. To see him was to intuit God's love.
So it must have been with St. John the evangelist, a man consumed,
even physically, with the love Christ died to reveal to us.

ST LUKE
Evangelist

1st Century

FEAST DAY
October 18th

PATRON SAINT
*doctors,
surgeons,
painters*

ATTRIBUTES
*gospel,
winged ox*

ST LUKE IS ONE of the four evangelists, the gospel writers. The medieval mind delighted in numbers, and since St. John had a vision of four winged creatures, and there were four gospels, each evangelist was given one of these creatures as his symbol. For St. Luke it was the winged ox because his gospel, and his alone, refers to the ox in the stable at Bethlehem. This is a wonderful image, an almost goofy ox, floating with a beatific smile above St. Luke, who sits bowed in thought pondering the mysteries of the life of Christ. The gospel scroll seems to be held by the ox, symbol of inspiration, but in front of St. Luke is a writing table, the other side of the story, because it is through the work and research and understanding of the evangelist that divine inspiration becomes actual and verbal. This brooding, prayerful St. Luke is an appealing image of the attentive waiting on God that we call prayer.

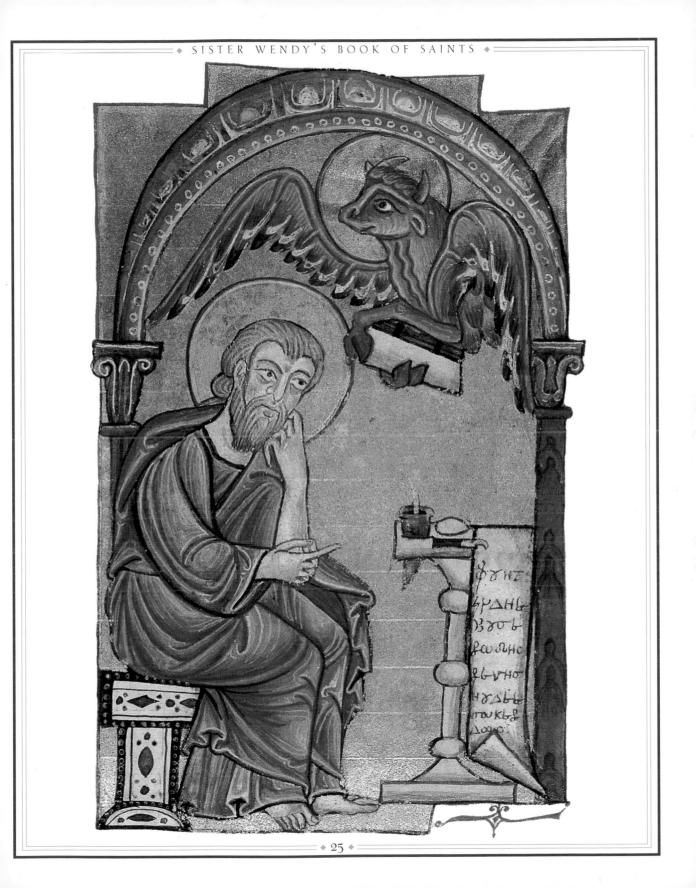

ST. MARY MAGDALENE
Follower of Christ

1st Century

FEAST DAY
July 22nd

PATRON SAINT
*hairdressers,
perfumiers,
gardeners,
prostitutes*

ATTRIBUTES
*jar of ointment,
long, loose hair,
crown of thorns,
mirror*

THE GOSPELS TELL US that Mary Magdalene, "out of whom the Lord had cast seven devils," was one of the faithful women at the foot of the cross and was present again at his tomb on Easter Sunday, to anoint him. Her jar of ointment is always with her, that sweet sign of love and repentance. She stands before us here, delicate and silent, hands clasped in prayer. It is not to us that she turns those big eyes, but to the Risen Lord whose love completely engrossed her. She has turned her back upon the city and its comforts. Beneath her feet is stony ground, where a desert plant almost miraculously flowers, a sign that the hardness of her previous life has been transformed. The legend says she withdrew to the desert, and when her garments decayed, was clad only in her long hair. She looks so frail and girlish, yet St. Mary Magdalene is the great example of the sinner whom grace can change into a saint. She still grieves over having wounded her Lord, though now she has been given a halo.

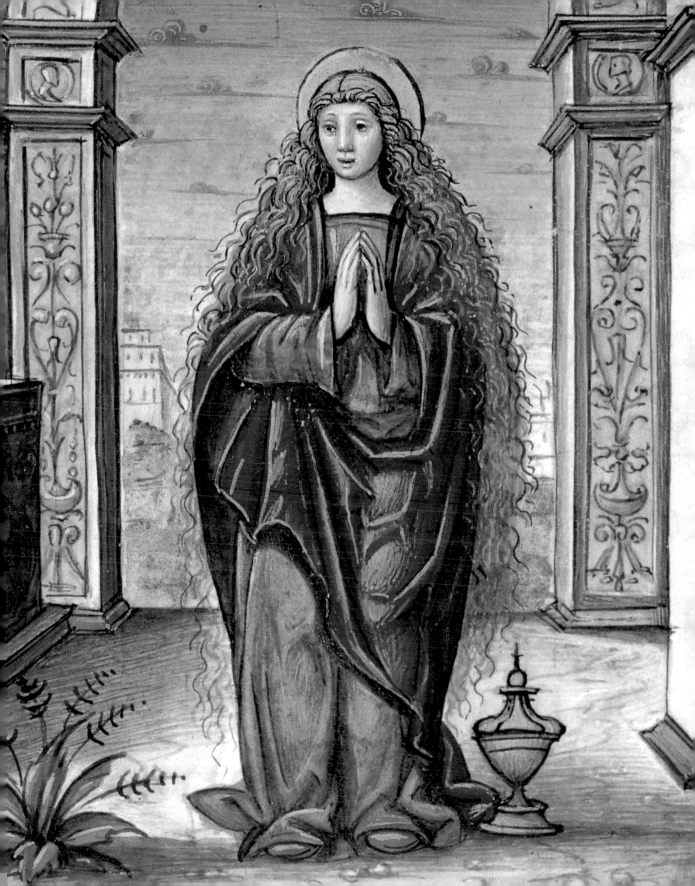

ST. PAUL
Apostle of the Gentiles

c.3–c.66

FEAST DAY
June 29th

PATRON SAINT
*tent–makers,
saddlers,
missionaries*

ATTRIBUTES
sword, book

THERE NEVER WAS a more dramatic conversion than that of St. Paul, so much so that it has passed into a saying: "a Damascus experience." Saul (the name Paul used while still a Jew) was an ardent persecutor of the Christians — ardent because he truly believed that this new faith was a heresy, hateful to the God he worshiped. While traveling to Damascus to attack the Christians there, he was violently hurled from his horse. He had a vision of Jesus, asking him why he was persecuting him, rebuking him, and demanding a change of heart. With a blinding insight Paul understood that his mind had been closed to the truth. He was not used to Christ, and so he had never really looked at him. Paul was, for a time, literally blinded, as this picture shows, flung to the ground, in literal and symbolic humiliation. From this he rose to faith, accepting his shame and using it. Even the splendid horse neighs in alarm, as Christ appears from heaven to change Paul's life. He could have sulked, he could have clung to his dignity. Instead, Paul took his overthrow with gratitude and became the greatest apostle the world has ever known.

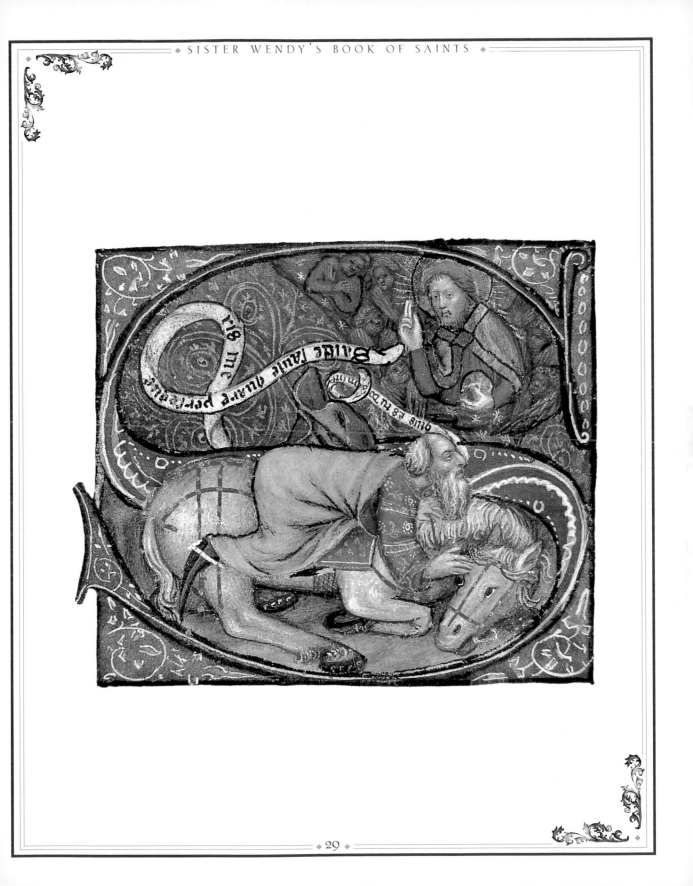

ST. PAUL
Apostle of the Gentiles

c.3–c.66

FEAST DAY
June 29th

PATRON SAINT
*tent-makers,
saddlers,
missionaries*

ATTRIBUTES
sword, book

ST PAUL TELLS US quite a lot about himself in his Epistles. We hear that he felt baffled by the way he acted, not doing what he knew was right, because "the spirit is willing but the flesh is weak." He tells us, mysteriously, that he was humiliated by a "sting of the flesh," which some commentators think might be epilepsy. Yet how dominant and single-minded he appears in St. Luke's Acts of the Apostles, a saint who truly knew how to use what he called "the sword of the Spirit," who spoke of Jesus with the most tender love. Still, he remains for most of us a rather remote figure, and that is how this artist sees him. He stands alone, his holy sword at rest, a great teacher with his book at hand. He makes us feel something of the cost of sanctity, its refusal to take time off, to slump, to be selfish. The lighthearted touch of the greyhound chasing the hare, beneath the picture of the saint, has a charming relevance. That dog will not let go: neither, in his chase for holiness, would St. Paul.

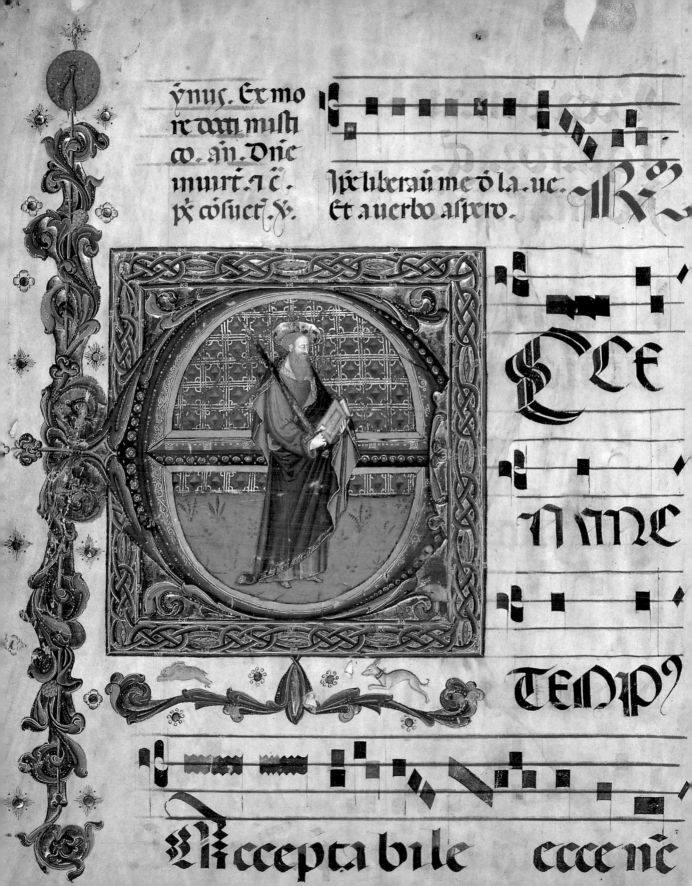

ST. JOHN *the* BAPTIST
Herald of the Messiah

died c.30

FEAST DAY
June 24th

PATRON SAINT
*Turin, Genoa,
Florence, baptism*

ATTRIBUTES
*lamb,
camelskin or
sheepskin tunic*

S ALOME DANCING SO AS to destroy St. John the Baptist is a common theme in art. But here we have a wholly different scene. Against a dark sky, St. John bows his head for the executioner, but Salome, in her moment of triumph, turns away forlorn. Has she just realized what she has done?

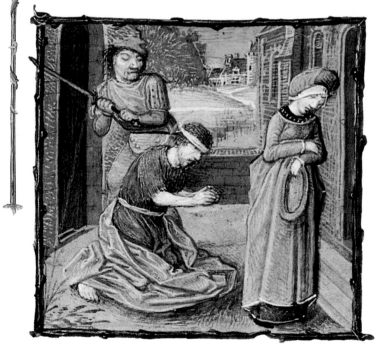

It is an extraordinary picture, and although, of course, it is primarily about St. John, it might also be about St. Salome, the saint-to-be, the woman this girl could grow into if she faces up to her tyrannical mother and takes her life into her own hands. She cannot bear to watch the consequences of her excited request to her royal uncle. She has used power irresponsibly, hardly aware that it is power. Now, too late, she sees it and grieves. For St. John, paradoxically, death means freedom. The golden fields outside the prison symbolize the heaven to which he is immediately bound, with peace and joy. St. John does not even see the unhappy girl; he is intent upon his God, resolved to die with great dignity.

ST STEPHEN
First martyr

died c.35

FEAST DAY
December 26th

PATRON SAINT
*deacons,
bricklayers*

ATTRIBUTE
stones

STEPHEN WAS THE FIRST MARTYR, one of the seven deacons of Jerusalem in the time of the apostles. Summoned to the Sanhedrin (Jewish council) to defend himself against the charge of blasphemy, he spoke with such passionate faith that the Sanhedrin was incensed. St. Stephen, young and tactless, annoyed them all the more by telling them they were "stiff-necked" resisters of the Holy Spirit.

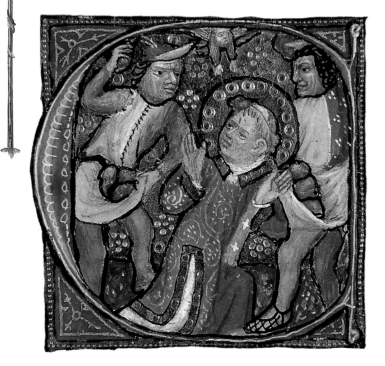

He was rushed outside the city walls to be stoned, crying out in rapture that he could actually see the heavens open and Christ standing at the Father's side. What makes this first martyrdom so beautiful is his final prayer, begging God: "Lay not this sin to their charge." It is a very levelheaded prayer, despite his earlier rhetoric. What they are doing is indeed a sin, killing anyone for his religious beliefs, but St. Stephen prays for no punishment to fall on them. Might he have felt he had provoked them? Here St. Stephen provides a lovely contrast to the malicious stone-throwers; he is already bleeding and visibly dying, yet his fair and youthful face seems irradiated with peace and steadfast hope. Totally unseen by the villains, a tiny blue angel at the top of the picture stretches out welcoming arms as the saint, arms lifted in prayer, prepares to join his Redeemer in the heavens.

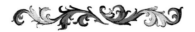

ST BARBARA
Virgin martyr

died c.200

FEAST DAY
December 4th

PATRON SAINT
*artillerymen,
architects,
miners*

ATTRIBUTES
*three–windowed
tower, lightning*

ST BARBARA IS ALWAYS portrayed with her tower, that fortress in which she was imprisoned by her despotic father, who was determined she should be protected from the contagion of Christianity. A wiser man would have known that this was the worst way to go about it. St. Barbara longed all the more to discover this strange new faith and, of course, she did. Her father seems to have been a genuinely cruel man. He denounced her to the emperor and offered to behead her himself. She was taken up a mountain and her father swung the ax. As it came down, lightning struck and killed him, which has made this gentle young aristocrat the patron saint of artillerymen. Here she sits contemplatively before her tower, bowing her head submissively to martyrdom.

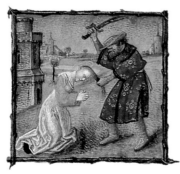

The point of her story is surely that no human endeavor, no "ivory tower," can hold us back from the intense dynamism of the faith. Even if we die for it we have lived and will live for ever.

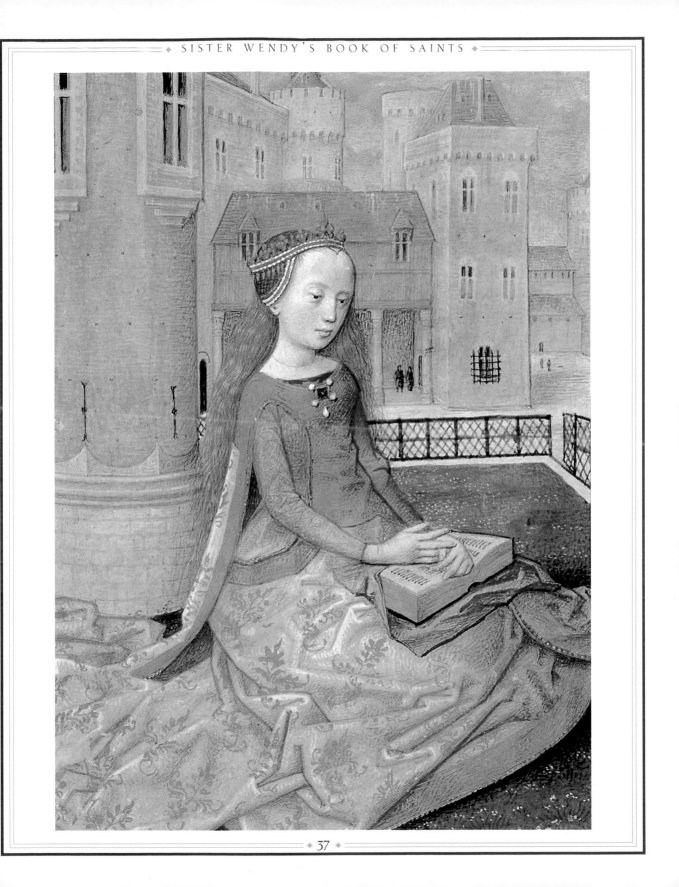

ST APOLLONIA

Virgin martyr

died 249

FEAST DAY
February 9th

PATRON SAINT
*dentists and
toothache*

ATTRIBUTES
teeth, pincers

ST APOLLONIA IS SITTING pensively in her cloister, holding her terrible emblem — teeth. But the artist, Jean Bourdichon (c.1457–1521), is taking liberties with the facts of history. The teeth are true enough, but the real St. Apollonia never knew the peace of a quiet convent and was far from young. She was, in fact, an aged deaconess of Alexandria, a tough old Egyptian lady who valiantly refused to

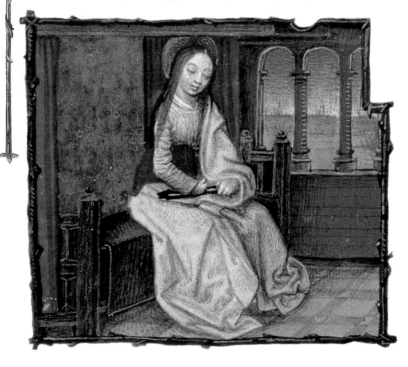

worship false gods when attacked by a mob rioting against the Christians. They hit her in the face so often and so fiercely that they knocked out all her teeth. **S**he is now the patron saint of toothache and dentists. Old and in pain, she still resisted stoutly. The mob lit a fire and threatened to throw her in unless she denied her faith. St. Apollonia asked for a moment's reflection, not because she intended submission, but because she was determined to spare them the sin of killing her. **W**hile they waited she stepped forward and threw herself into the flames, accepting the inevitable but in a way that might help her persecutors to think more deeply. It is this spirit of sensitive courage that Bourdichon gets right, even if only symbolically.

S⸗ AGATHA
Virgin martyr

died c.251

FEAST DAY
February 5th

PATRON SAINT
*Catania, breast
disorders,
bell-founders,
nurses*

ATTRIBUTES
*breasts in a dish
(often confused
with loaves
or bells)*

ST AGATHA IS ONE of the many early Christian martyrs, but the manner of her death has made her, for women at least, unforgettable. She was a girl of great beauty, as indeed this miniature shows. Agatha's misfortune was to attract the Roman prefect of Sicily, where she lived, at the foot of Mount Etna, and when she repulsed him, he had her sent to a brothel, to be degraded. The story says that nobody touched her, and the picture suggests the reason: for all her smiling serenity, this is a figure of awesome dignity. Thwarted, the prefect condemned her to death, but first he had — a shuddering thought — her breasts twisted off as she was hung upside down on a pillar. She holds them, pathetic lumps of severed flesh in a blood-filled dish, and gravely draws her mantle across the mutilation. All those who have had breast cancer will respond to her situation and her courage. They may have no choice, but neither, in her own mind, did she. She too was choosing life, at whatever cost, but for her it was eternal life.

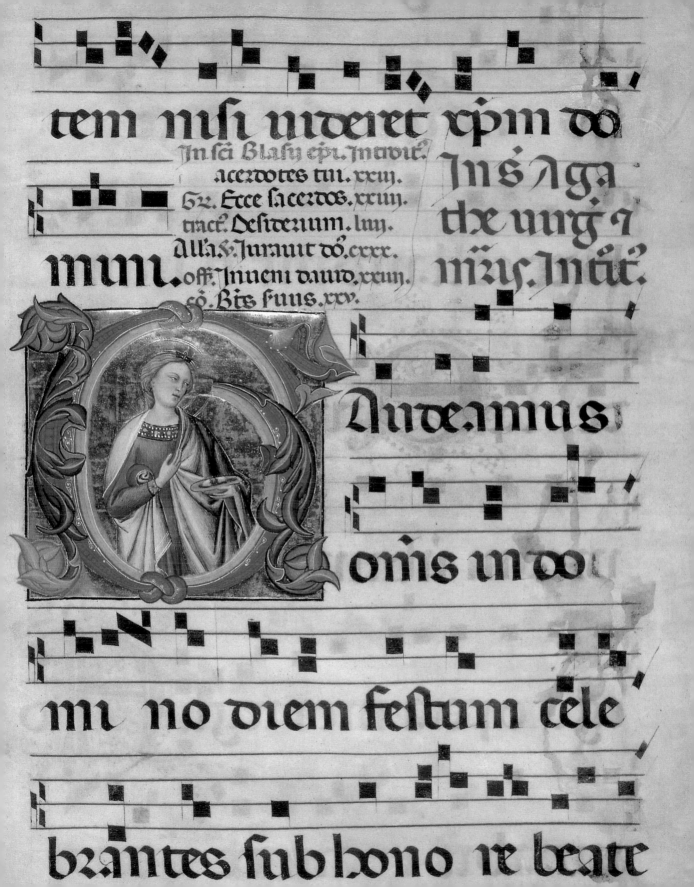

tem nisi uideret xpm do

In scã Blasij epi. Intdit.
acerdotes tui. xxiij.
Gr. Ecce sacerdos. xxiiij.
tract. Desiderium. luij.
Alla. v. Iurauit dõ. cxxx.
off. Inueni dauid. xxiij.
cõ. Bts tuus. xxv.

In s Aga
the uirg i
mris. Intut.

mun.

Audeamus

oms in do

mi no diem festum cele

brantes sub hono re beate

ST DOROTHY
Virgin martyr

died c.300/310

FEAST DAY
February 6th

PATRON SAINT
florists

ATTRIBUTE
laden basket

THIS ELEGANT YOUNG woman with her secret little smile is St. Dorothy, whose story touches upon the meaning of names. Her name means gift of God. As she was being led to her death to be beheaded she passed a young lawyer, Theophilus, a name that means lover of God. Unfortunately, Theophilus was not at all a God-lover but a young cynic. It exasperated him to see this silly woman, looking as sublimely content as she does here, going so pointlessly to her death, to the Christian Paradise (Paradise means garden). He jeered at her, and Dorothy, who knew, as he did not, that there is truly a Paradise, said she would send him flowers. It was bitter winter, but as she died, a child gave Theophilus a basket of apples and roses. Whereupon he did fulfill his name and soon followed her to Paradise. It is her dignified certainty that is so charming, or, if one does not believe, so irritating.

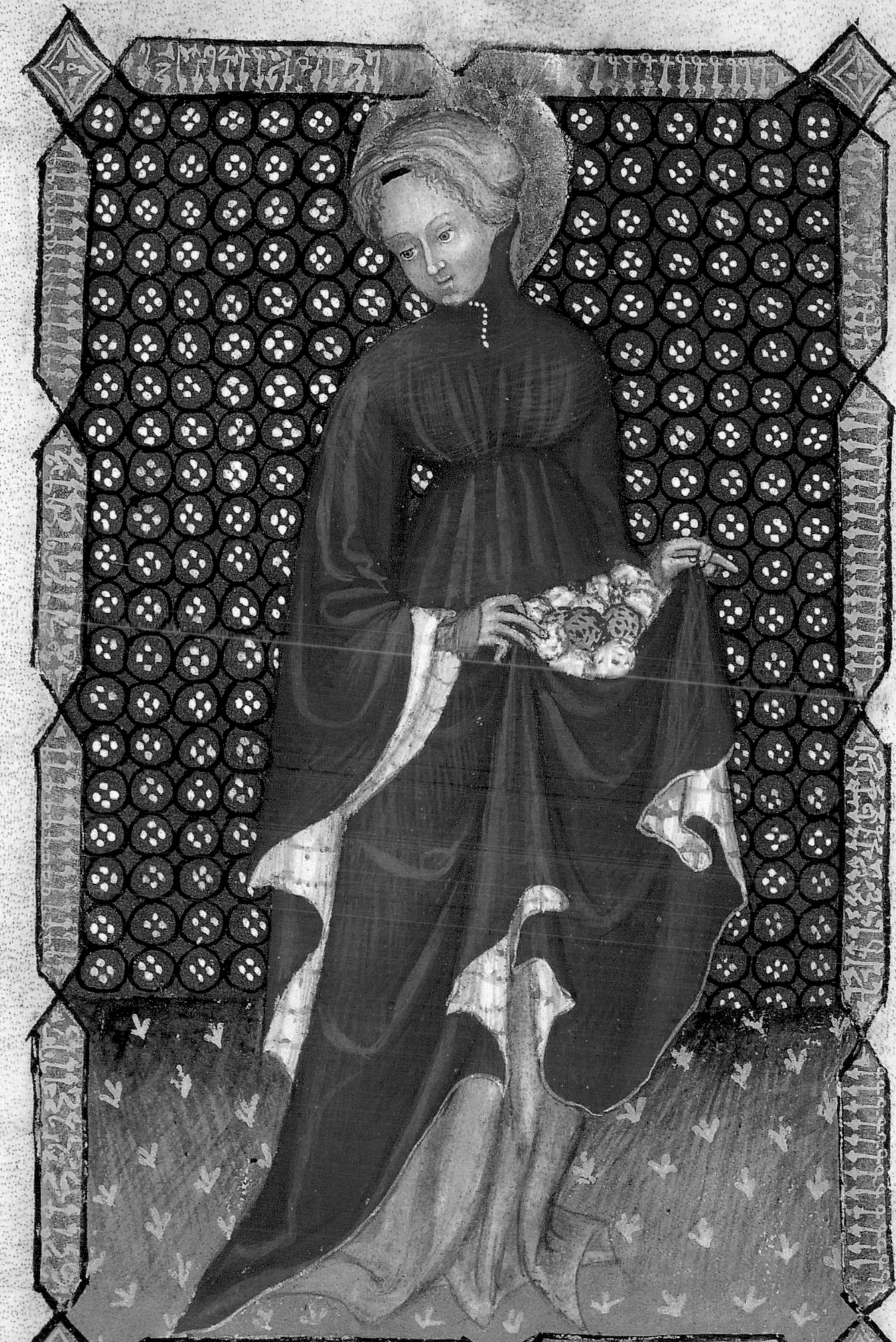

ST LUCY
Virgin martyr

died 304

FEAST DAY
December 13th

PATRON SAINT
eye diseases

ATTRIBUTES
*eyes dangling on
a stalk, lamp or
altar candles*

ST LUCY IS ONE of those saints whose legend seems to have been concocted from the meaning of her name. Lucy comes from the Latin *lux*, meaning light, and there is a wonderful golden gleam in the halo that surrounds her head and on the adornment of her cloak. But light in the Middle Ages had its primary connection with the eyes. It is the eyes that give us access to the material world, and we can see only in the light. More than that, even today we speak of the eyes as the windows of the soul, suggesting that there is two-way traffic: we can see out but also we can be seen into. Vision, after all, can be purely physical, or the word can be used to signify a mystical experience. People in the Middle Ages were also very conscious that there were two kinds of light, spiritual and physical, and that they were intimately connected. The Lucy story had as its horrific climax the removal of her eyes. She became eyeless, and yet she "saw" because her spiritual sight remained undimmed. Artists usually depicted her, unpleasantly, as either bearing her eyes on a plate, or dangling them from a stalk like two cherries.

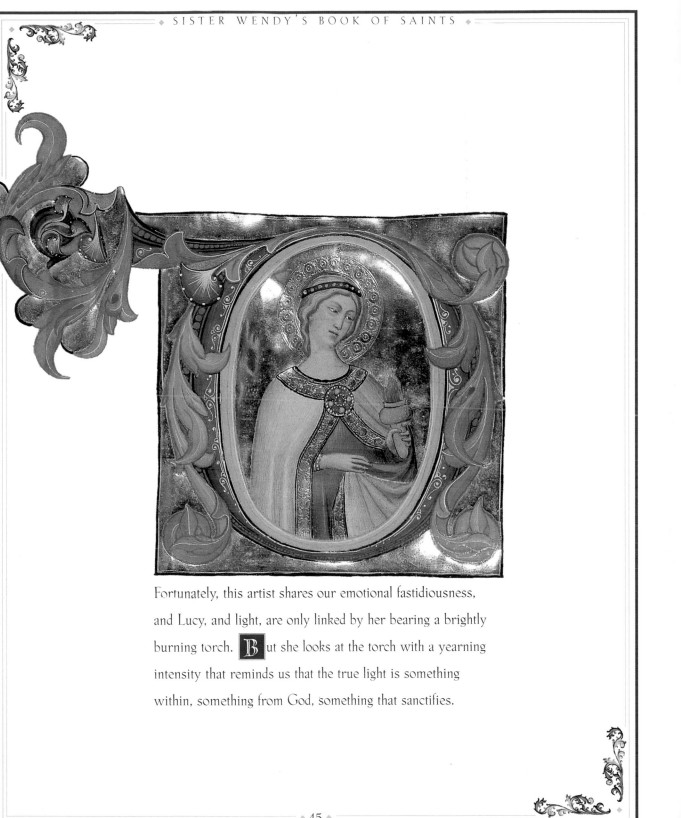

Fortunately, this artist shares our emotional fastidiousness, and Lucy, and light, are only linked by her bearing a brightly burning torch. **B**ut she looks at the torch with a yearning intensity that reminds us that the true light is something within, something from God, something that sanctifies.

ST CATHERINE of ALEXANDRIA
Virgin martyr

c.290–c.310

FEAST DAY
November 25th

PATRON SAINT
*philosophers,
scholars, millers,
spinners, clergy,
wheelwrights,
young girls*

ATTRIBUTE
spiked wheel

ST CATHERINE IS COMMEMORATED in the Catherine wheel, that sparkling firework that spins merrily around. It was anything but merry in reality, a terrible spiked wheel, which we can see being readied for her in the background. She is that rare being, an intellectual woman saint, who challenged the emperor himself about idol worship, and when he sent fifty philosophers to argue with her, talked them all down and converted them. At this point, we begin to see that this is a legend, still more when the emperor begs Catherine to marry him and is told that she is already married, to Christ. He has her tied to the wheel, which bursts apart, and then she is beheaded and carried by angels to Mount Sinai. Legend or not, her story speaks to us of the wisdom of the faith, of how it can triumph over intellectualism, over seductions to glory, and over fear. St. Catherine tramples the political power of the state under foot, not scornfully but sadly. We feel she would have loved to convert the wicked emperor. She is crowned — a princess — and she rests upon the sword of her martyrdom and the book of her salvation.

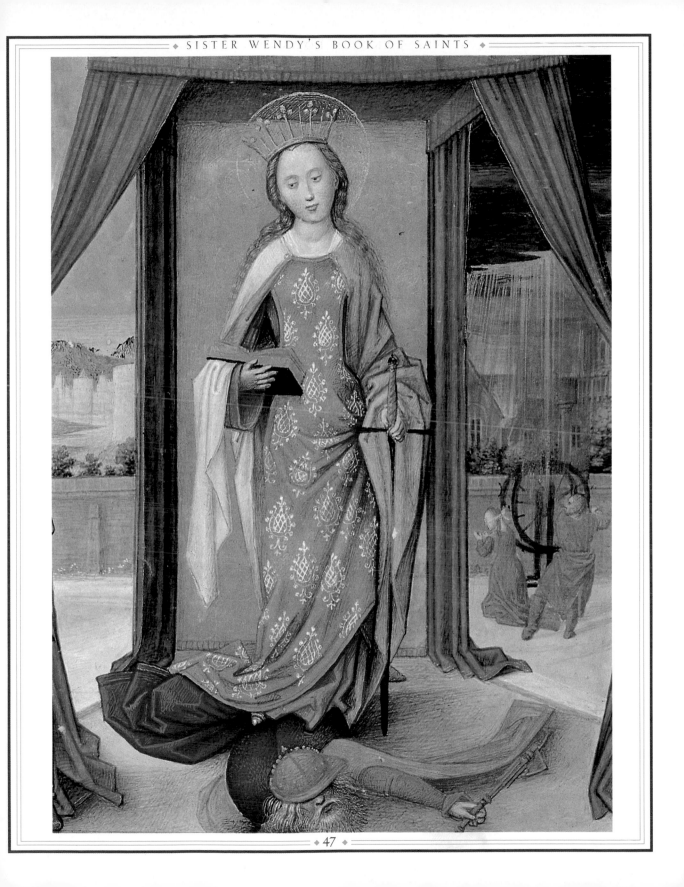

ST LAWRENCE

Martyr

died 258

FEAST DAY
August 10th

PATRON SAINT
cooks, libraries

ATTRIBUTE
grill

ST LAWRENCE IS AN extraordinarily interesting saint because he comes right from the beginning of Christianity, and often it is hard to grasp the personality of those early saints; they are distant and we do not know enough about them. We only know two stories about St. Lawrence and both illustrate the same quirky, courageous, humorous character for which he is renowned. One story about St. Lawrence is that when the pope, to whom he was deacon, was arrested, he gave Lawrence all the books of the church and all their treasures. Lawrence hid the books, which is why he is patron saint of libraries (whether for hiding or keeping you can work out for yourself). But he sold the treasures — a good example — and gave the money to the poor. When the prefect of Rome demanded from him the church's treasures, St. Lawrence did not say what he had done with them, he merely asked for three days to collect them. Then, with that same sardonic wit that is his characteristic, he presented

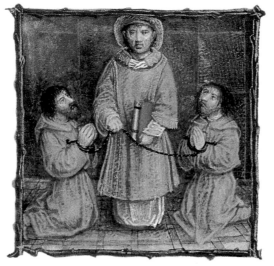

to the prefect all the down-and-outs of Rome, all the poor widows and orphans, all the sick and helpless. He raised an eyebrow at the prefect's expostulations: "These," he insisted, "are the church's treasures, the poor of Christ." He stands here in his deacon's robes, flanked by two representative poor men, whom he has taught to pray and helped to keep hopeful. One can see why the authorities feared him.

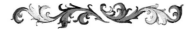

ST LAWRENCE
Martyr

died 258

FEAST DAY
August 10th

PATRON SAINT
cooks, libraries

ATTRIBUTE
grill

ST LAWRENCE IS ALWAYS seen as he is here, with a grill (a grate for broiling food), because the emperor commanded that he should be executed by being roasted alive. The artist who painted this striking picture makes us see it in horrid and graphic detail. St. Lawrence is famous for the peace with which he endured so horrible a fate. It was more than peace: it was a time when he showed to the full his extraordinary sense of humor. We see three executioners, all of whom are absolutely hideous, pouring on the coals, pumping up the bellows, holding him down. Lawrence lies there, cooking (it is difficult to imagine the pain he must be suffering), and yet he calls after them, "I think I'm done on this side, why not turn me over?" To be able to jest when one is in such agony is not just courage. It bespeaks a serenity that can come only from complete trust in God. It is that kind of wit, a sort of personal encounter with the realities of life, that makes St. Lawrence very special.

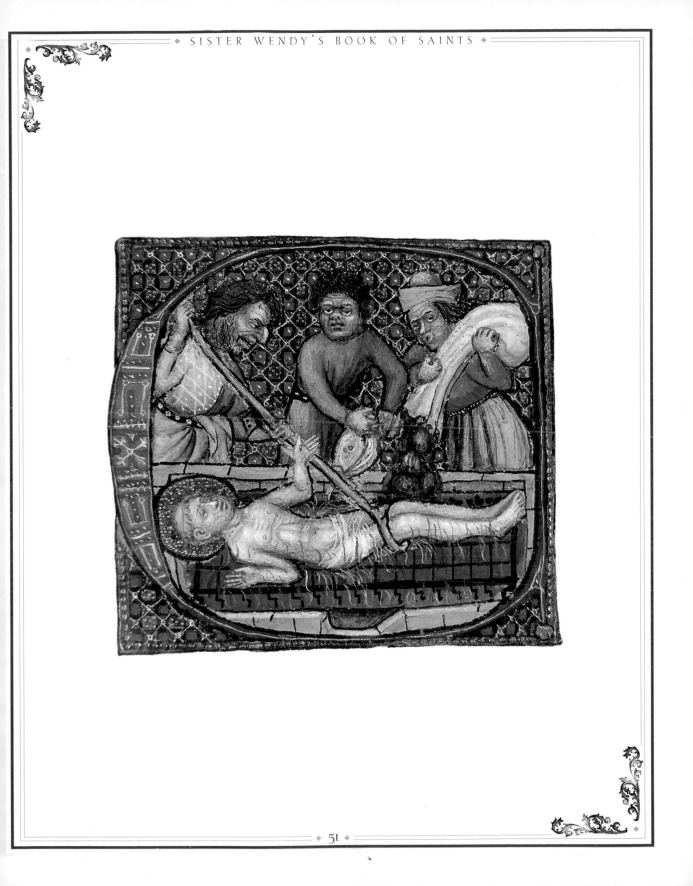

ST JEROME
Doctor of the church

c.341–420

FEAST DAY
September 30th

PATRON SAINT
*librarians,
translators*

ATTRIBUTES
*lion, cardinal's
hat, study*

FOR MANY CENTURIES St. Jerome was the most popular saint in art. There are many images of him in his study translating the Bible, a massive work of scholarship for which he became justly renowned. But scholars are sometimes irascible men, who do not suffer fools gladly, and there are just as many images of St. Jerome on his knees in the desert, praying and repenting. This charming miniature shows his hands folded peacefully on his bosom, a position to which they were not accustomed. On the margins swirl phantasmal creatures, perhaps in reference to the horrifying hallucinations that sometimes came upon him in his nights of prayer. But there is comfort here, too; at his feet crouches the legendary lion. The saint is said to have diagnosed the animal's ferocity as the simple effect of a thorn in his paw. Always fearless, St. Jerome advanced on the lion, removed the thorn, and secured a lasting friend and admirer. Perhaps they found they had much in common? St. Jerome tamed the lion, and the love of God tamed St. Jerome.

ST PAULA

Woman saint

died 404

FEAST DAY
January 26th

PATRON SAINT
widows

ATTRIBUTE
*usually depicted
with St. Jerome
(see opposite)*

ST PAULA WAS neither a virgin nor a martyr, but a contented society widow whose luxurious life was transformed by St. Jerome. She was so struck by what he made her understand about Christ, and the need to serve him with a whole heart, that when he left Rome for the Holy Land, she followed him with her adult daughter and some friends to set up a convent and live in austerity. **S**he studied Greek and Hebrew; her demure bearing conceals a ferocious need to understand. St. Jerome was a difficult man, however saintly, so it was spiritual need alone that impelled St. Paula to her arduous life. Of course, she attracted gossip and misunderstanding, but nothing could deflect her from her longing to come closer to Christ, in his poor, in his teachings, in himself.

ST AMBROSE
Doctor of the church

c.339–c.397

FEAST DAY
December 7th

PATRON SAINT
*Milan,
beekeepers*

ATTRIBUTES
*beehive,
three–tailed
whip*

ST AMBROSE PRESENTS a confusing personal image. He was one of those natural leaders, an instinctive man of power and eloquence, who seems to ascend effortlessly into positions of supreme importance. In fact, when he was voted into the role of Bishop of Milan, he had not been baptized, let alone ordained a priest. What people were responding to was his air of authority. They responded wisely: it was not an empty authority. He had a brilliant intellect and great powers of eloquence. In other words, St. Ambrose was a born politician.

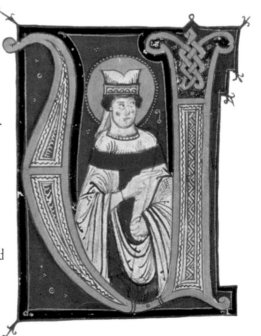

Yet his whole life was devoted to the living of Christian virtues, especially humility and charity. If he verbally scourged emperors and heretics it was — we hope — for the noblest of reasons. It is hard to see him straight. He rode two horses, and the only indication that he rode both triumphantly was that both his political influence and his deep spirituality astonished his contemporaries. Here he holds a book to indicate his great learning and perhaps also his gift for poetry: some of his hymns are still sung in church. But he looks out at us rather sadly, a bishop, a doctor of the church, and a man much burdened by undesired responsibility.

ST AUGUSTINE

Doctor of the church

354–430

FEAST DAY
August 28th

PATRON SAINT
*theologians,
printers*

ATTRIBUTES
*child with shell;
pierced, broken,
or flaming heart*

I N THE GREAT capital "G" that begins his book on the most glorious City of God, St. Augustine kneels with his back to us, his bishop's miter on the ground, rapt in prayer. He is praying to the Holy Trinity — merciful Father, crucified Son, light-bringing Holy Spirit — as they glimmer before him in a vision. The magnificent page is bordered with figures and incidents, as it must be when we remember that this saint, unusually, wrote his autobiography — and called it his Confessions. Y et what was always central to St. Augustine, that learned and subtle thinker, was precisely this mystery, the Trinity. The small child with the bowl in the upper left-hand corner must refer to the famous story of St. Augustine's walk along the shore. He saw a child intently running to and from the sea, each time filling a shell with water and pouring it into a hole in the sand. St. Augustine, who had an illegitimate but dearly loved son, asked the child what he was doing. The answer was, "pouring the sea into my hole." When St. Augustine kindly explained the impossibility of it, the child retorted that it was just

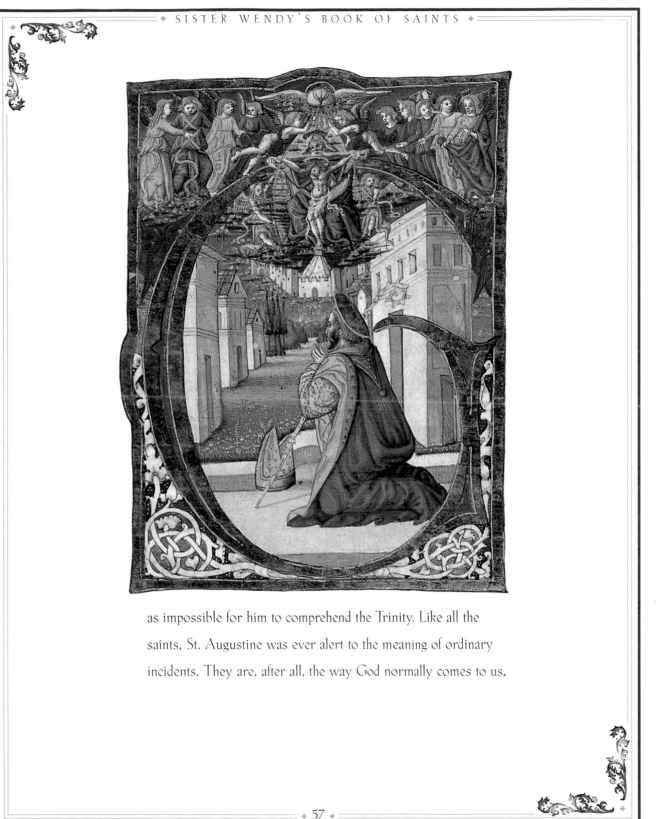

as impossible for him to comprehend the Trinity. Like all the
saints, St. Augustine was ever alert to the meaning of ordinary
incidents. They are, after all, the way God normally comes to us.

ST AUGUSTINE
Doctor of the church

354–430

FEAST DAY
August 28th

PATRON SAINT
*theologians,
brewers,
printers*

ATTRIBUTES
*child with shell;
a pierced,
broken, or
flaming heart*

ST AUGUSTINE WAS ONE of those rare and extraordinary beings we call a genius. His theological teachings still influence contemporary thought. His powerful personality dominated his era, and his intense love of God made him the model of what it means to be a saint. Yet we feel close to this saint, who in his wild youth prayed for chastity, "but not yet," and so humbly accepted that his love of God would always leave him yearning: "You have us for Yourself, O God, and our hearts are restless until they rest in You." These two pictures, by very different artists, could almost be a "before" and "after" of the saint. The seated Augustine, young, handsome, hopeful, is clearly just beginning his great career as bishop. The halo is there, but it is his humanity that strikes us. The standing St. Augustine is austere. Penance and labor have worn him to the bone, and

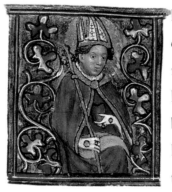

he seems remote from the warmth of earthly passions. But he is not remote from divine passions: he holds up a fragile hand in blessing, and with the other holds out to us his book on the City of God.

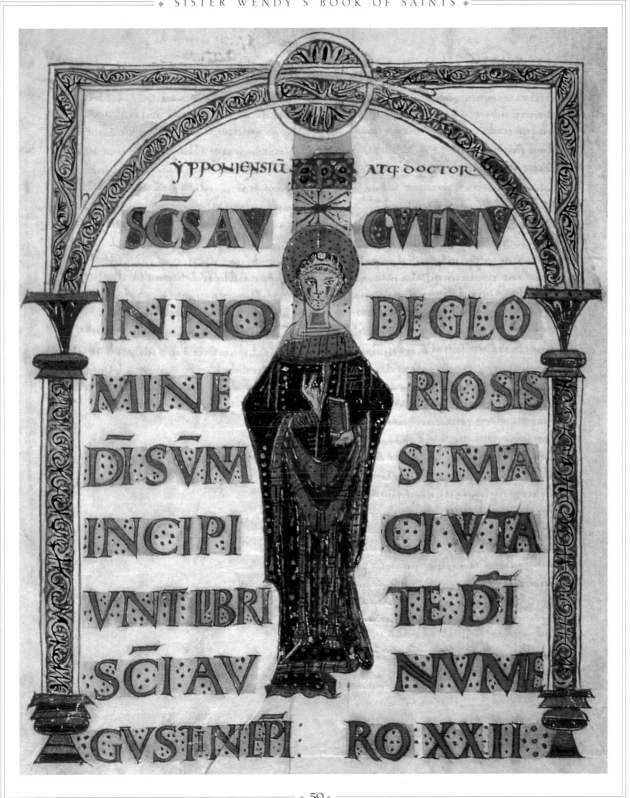

ST GREGORY

Doctor of the church and pope

c.540–c.604

FEAST DAY
September 3rd

PATRON SAINT
*masons,
singers,
musicians,
teachers*

ATTRIBUTES
*masons,
papal crozier,
singers,
papal tiara,
dove*

ST GREGORY WAS ONE of the truly great popes, despite the fact (or should it be because of it) that he was profoundly reluctant to accept the office. He was a monk who felt he needed the peace and prayerfulness of his monastery; he was in fact the first monk ever to become a pope. Perhaps the immense authority with which he ruled the church came from this same prayerfulness. He was a learned man, passionately consumed by the desire that priests should be not learned as such, but theologically learned. He understood that a priest was there to serve, and it was Gregory who described the role of pope as "servant of the servants of God." A good priest, a good bishop, a good pope, is precisely that, a servant, because Jesus spoke of himself as being "among you as one who serves." Gregory was also a great missionary, at least in desire, and he persuaded St. Augustine (*see pp.56–59*) to take the long and dangerous journey to a very remote part of the Roman Empire to convert the English, and hence become St. Augustine of Canterbury.

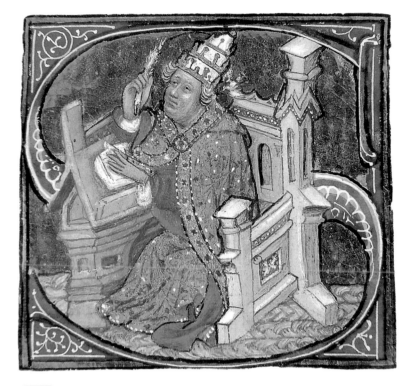

This picture shows Gregory composing one of his many books. He has a wise old face, heavy and benign, lifting his quill pen heavenward in a silent appeal for the divine inspiration that never failed him: at his ear hovers the silvery whiteness of the Holy Spirit in the form of a dove. He is hemmed in by the massive papal throne and weighed down by the massive papal tiara, yet his brow is radiantly serene.

ST. THOMAS AQUINAS

Doctor of the church — Dominican

1225–1274

FEAST DAY
January 28th

PATRON SAINT
*academics,
philosophers,
theologians,
booksellers,
colleges,
universities*

ATTRIBUTES
ox, chalice, star

IF BRILLIANCE IS the power to absorb a great many facts and theories and make sense of them, imposing an elegant and comprehensible order, then humanity has never known a greater mind than that of St. Thomas Aquinas. He did not look clever. When he escaped his aristocratic family to become a lowly Dominican brother, much to their chagrin, he was known as "the dumb ox," being very large and very silent. A compassionate fellow novice undertook to explain theology lessons to him, and the saint accepted gratefully. Only if his young instructor faltered in explanation did St. Thomas humbly suggest a way forward, until it slowly dawned upon them all what kind of genius St. Thomas was. All our insights into the faith have been affected by him, by his grasp of fundamentals and his intense prayer. He left his great *Summa Theologica* unfinished, saying it seemed like "so much straw," compared with what the Holy Spirit had taught him in prayer. For these mystical experiences there are no words, not even for a genius. Even so, all his words, stemming from what cannot be said, point us toward this silent wisdom.

Sancti Thome de Aquino ordinis predicatorum super quarto libro sententiarum preclarum opus feliciter incipit.

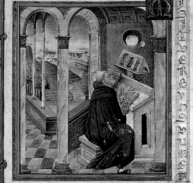

ST CATHERINE of SIENA

Doctor of the church — Dominican

1347–1380

FEAST DAY
April 29th

PATRON SAINT
Italy

ATTRIBUTES
stigmata, lily

IN TODAY'S OVERPOPULATED world, it is doubtful whether St. Catherine would have been born: she was the youngest of a family of twenty-five children. She was to become the most powerful woman of the fourteenth century; in fact, one of the most powerful women of any century. From childhood this lively and attractive girl longed only to love and serve God with a passionate abandon that can almost seem obsessive. Her fame spread, to the extent that popes and kings trembled at her frown. Obviously, hers was a temperament of immense charismatic power, and it was all directed, selflessly, to the service of God and the church. Her definition of God is still effective: "God is He who is, and I am she who is not." But her fervor led her to live unwisely, neither eating nor sleeping, and she died, exhausted by prayer, when she was only thirty-three. The artist felt he needed two images: the woman of great prayer, and the woman of great action.

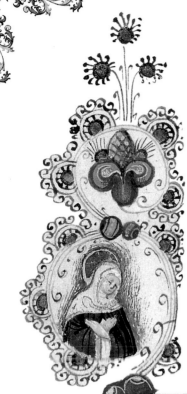

Above is Catherine in ecstasy, in her black–and–white Dominican habit; below is Catherine holding the book of her teaching and the lily of her purity, with the black and white of her habit stark against a scarlet background. **S**he could neither read nor write, but she dictated her messages, often using several secretaries at the same time. Perhaps the little image at the foot of the page, where one figure whispers

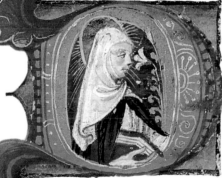

in another's ear, refers to her fame, carried by word of mouth. She was loved and revered, deeply human and yet transparently a lover of God.

ST ANTHONY ABBOT
Hermit

251–356

FEAST DAY
January 17th

PATRON SAINT
basket-makers

ATTRIBUTES
*pig,
T-shaped staff,
bell*

ANTHONY ABBOT IS the most famous of the desert fathers. He lived life in the desert to its incredible fullness, not eating, not sleeping, having the most terrible hallucinations. These hallucinations, which nearly sent him insane, were of beautiful, naked women surrounding him. Here they are with their fancy hats, and as you can see, poor St. Anthony does not know how to cope. He is backing away in horrified desperation. The naked women are advancing in a purposeful kind of way. They were not, of course, real naked women, they were the machinations of the devil. Another one of the other lovely stories about St. Anthony was that he began to get temptations to pride: that he was the greatest saint in the desert. A heavenly voice said to him, "No, there is a greater."

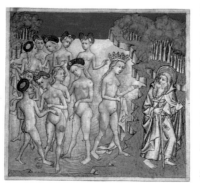

So Anthony set out to find him, and the greater saint was Paul the Hermit. When they met, these two old men, who had given their lives to Christ, simply fell into each other's arms, hugging and kissing.

E ach was delighted to see somebody who loved God even more than he himself did. There is a little miracle attached to this, in that every day a raven used to bring Paul the Hermit half a loaf of bread. On the day when St. Anthony was visiting, the raven brought a whole loaf and the two of them broke bread together, because even a desert father needs a friend. In fact, we could say that being a friend is part of being a saint.

ST. ANTHONY ABBOT
Hermit

251–356

FEAST DAY
January 17th

PATRON SAINT
basket-makers

ATTRIBUTES
*pig,
T-shaped staff,
bell*

THIS IS A MAJESTIC ST. ANTHONY, framed against a picturesque background that perhaps suggests the life he has forsaken. Yet he spent his days alone in the desert, with only the pig now remaining to remind us of his terrible temptations there. The mild and biddable pig was once the devil himself, a ferocious fiend determined to seduce the hermit from his solitary life of prayer. But St. Anthony tamed him and made him a companion, a piglet friend, which is highly encouraging to us all! One of the reasons why the saint had such frightening temptations was that he was determined to take seriously the biblical exhortation to "pray without ceasing," thinking it meant to do nothing else. But in a dream an angel advised him to work as well, that this was another form of prayer. When St. Anthony pointed out that there was no work in the Egyptian desert, the angel tartly told him to climb a palm tree, collect the leaves, and weave them into mats. This sensible advice gave his life the balance it had needed. There is no point in giving God what he is not asking, and the human mind needs to "pray always," but in different ways.

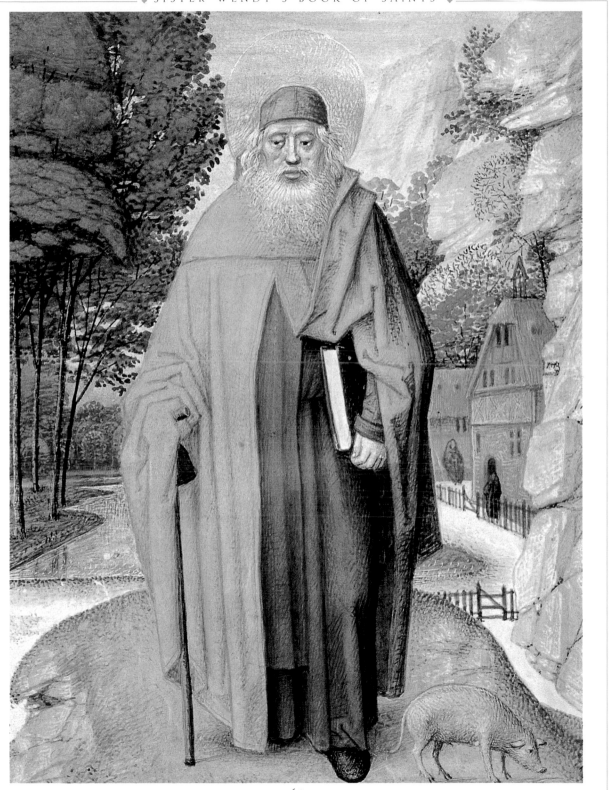

ST MARTIN of TOURS
Apostle of the Gauls

c.316–c.400

FEAST DAY
November 11th

PATRON SAINT
*France, soldiers,
drapers, furriers,
tailors*

ATTRIBUTES
*cloak, Roman
soldier's uniform*

ST MARTIN HAS THE DISTINCTION of being the first Christian pacifist or, at least, the first we know about. He came from a military family and obediently followed his father into the emperor's legions, patrolling the frontiers. But when war broke out, St. Martin saw, young as he was, that it was a war of aggression, an unjust war, and he resigned his commission. He volunteered to walk in the vanguard carrying a cross, to be killed if need be, but he himself would not kill. The world was baffled by his behavior and still is: this episode is rarely portrayed. But we can all understand the story here. St. Martin meets a naked beggar. He gives him all he can, which is half his uniform cloak. That night, Christ appeared to him, wearing the half–cloak, saying, "My friend Martin gave me this." St. Martin was still a pagan at the time, but this incident led to his conversion and his dramatic refusal of worldly values. We are shown here, not the actual cutting of the cloak, but Martin's moment of decision. It seemed a smallish thing, to be improperly dressed as an officer for the sake of charity, but it changed his life.

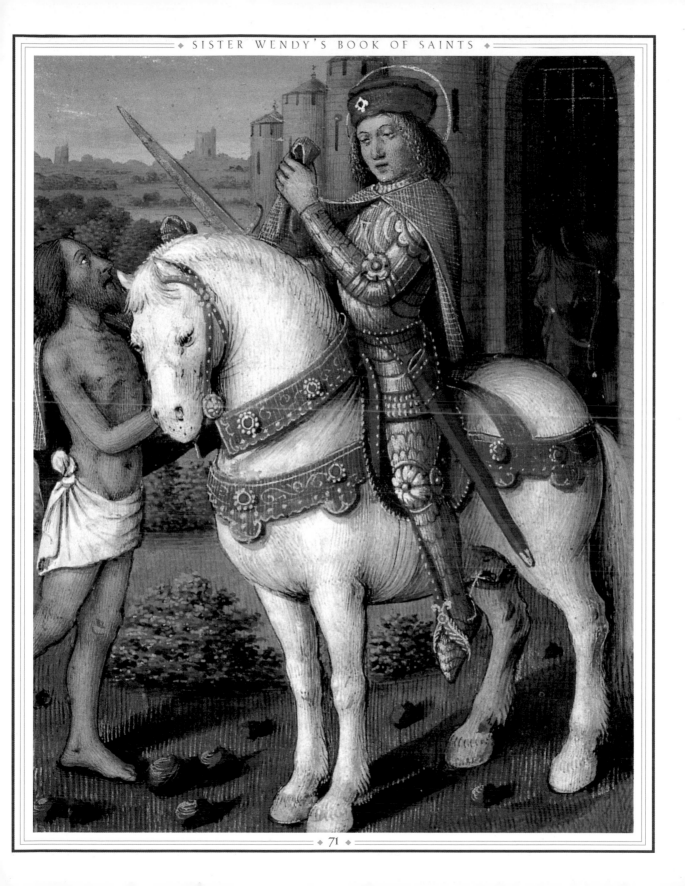

ST BENEDICT
Founder of Western monasticism

c.480–c.547

FEAST DAY
July 11th

PATRON SAINT
*Europe,
schoolchildren*

ATTRIBUTES
*broken cup,
rule book,
monastic
buildings*

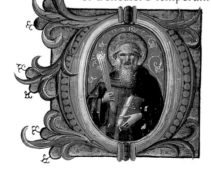

SINCE MANY OF THE MANUSCRIPTS of the medieval church were written and painted in Benedictine monasteries, it is not surprising that there are many illustrations of St. Benedict himself. For the monks, he was their holy founder; for the world at large, he was the civilizing influence that brought peace and stability to Europe. It was his Benedictine monks who copied (and so preserved) the ancient classics, who cultivated the wild countryside, and who showed all people an example of orderly and contented living. Order is the keynote of Benedict's temperament. He is a natural lawgiver, and here we see him holding the rule book and the lighted torch that illuminated Europe. One could not guess it, but this extraordinary person turned out to have a twin sister, St. Scholastica.

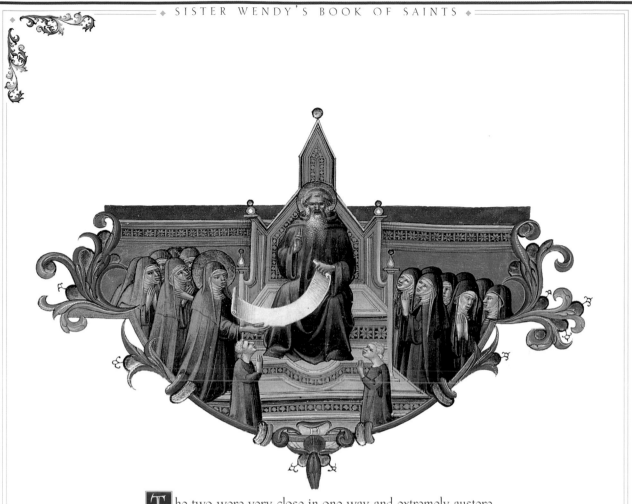

The two were very close in one way and extremely austere and self-denying in another. Benedict gave his rule — that blessed rule of peace and stability — to Scholastica and her Benedictine nuns. This picture commemorates that precious gift.

ST FRANCIS of ASSISI
Founder of the Franciscan order

1181–1226

FEAST DAY
October 4th

PATRON SAINT
*animals,
ecologists,
Italy,
Assisi, animal
welfare societies,*

ATTRIBUTES
*birds, deer,
stigmata*

THERE IS A RATHER cynical verse that says "To live with the saints above is heavenly, blessed, and glory, but to live with the saints on earth is a very different story." One saint about whom that could never be said was Francis because he was exactly what we think a saint ought to be: a completely loving spirit. In his *Canticle of the Creatures* he called upon "Brother Sun" and "Sister Moon" to praise God; he truly felt that everything that existed — from angels to rocks — was part of his dear family. He was also passionate in his espousal of poverty because then he was completely free to give himself in service. There are many stories about St. Francis, and he is frequently depicted in art preaching to the birds and the fish, but this delightful miniature shows Francis with the wolf of Gubbio. Legend has it that a man-eating wolf was terrorizing the people of Gubbio. Francis said there was no need to kill it, instead he would go to the forest and reason with the wolf.

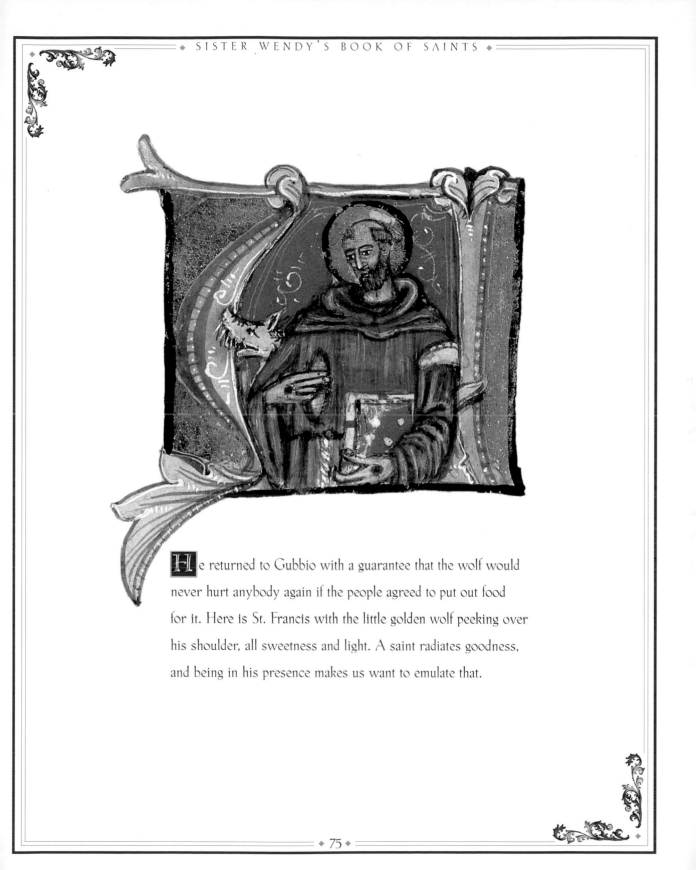

He returned to Gubbio with a guarantee that the wolf would never hurt anybody again if the people agreed to put out food for it. Here is St. Francis with the little golden wolf peeking over his shoulder, all sweetness and light. A saint radiates goodness, and being in his presence makes us want to emulate that.

ST THOMAS À BECKET
Bishop and martyr

1118–1170

FEAST DAY
December 29th

PATRON SAINT
Canterbury

ATTRIBUTES
*sword in
his skull,
death at an altar*

ST THOMAS À BECKET WAS ONE of those rare saints who died for political principle: he strongly believed that church and state must remain separate. King Henry II had been his closest friend and had persuaded St. Thomas, against his will, to become Archbishop of Canterbury. Later, when the saint refused to obey him in church matters, the King, in his rage, cursed so recklessly that four knights set off at once to teach this upstart priest his place. They cut him down in his own cathedral, and the whole of Europe shuddered at the sacrilege. This is not a very vigorous cutting–down, the two knights we see look apathetic and have wholly imbecilic expressions. Historically we can explain this, as it was a lunatic act to take the King's drunken ravings against his friend seriously. St. Thomas, though, dies with grace and dignity, offering his life with open hands to God. This heroic death, his refusing to escape even though it might have been possible, did more for the cause of the faith than St. Thomas could have imagined. Within a mere three years he was canonized, a martyr of conscience whose example is always relevant.

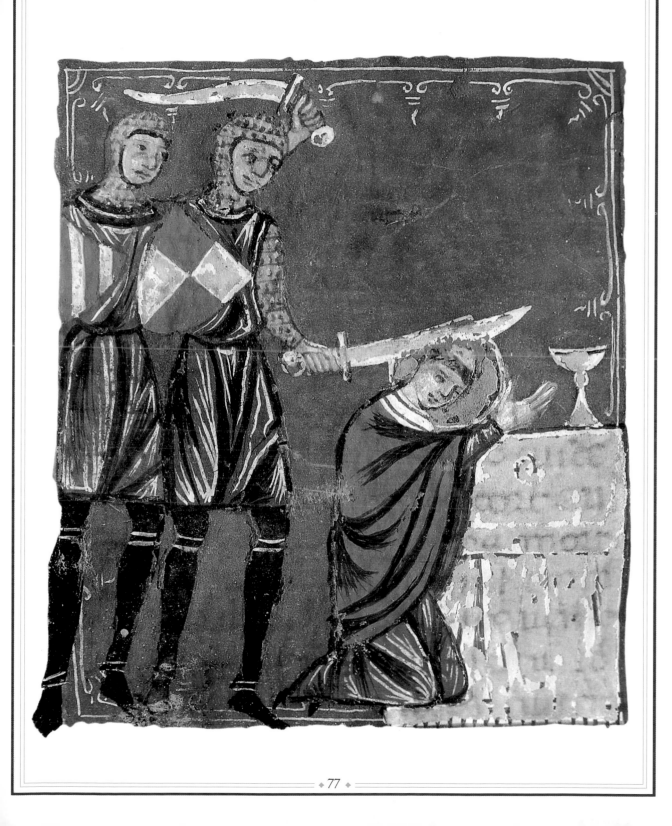

ST CHRISTOPHER
The Christ-bearer

3rd Century

FEAST DAY
July 25th

PATRON SAINT
*travelers,
motorists*

ATTRIBUTE
*Christ child on
shoulders*

ST CHRISTOPHER WOULD BE dismayed to know that even those who do not believe in God believe superstitiously in him, as the patron saint of travelers. His medallion is in many a vehicle and, generous man that he was, perhaps he does indeed protect the drivers of the world. For himself, he walked everywhere and especially through rivers, where he was a ferryman. But it was a unique ferrying. St. Christopher, in an age when most men were relatively small, was immensely tall — a giant. So he often carried people across the waters on his back. His story is

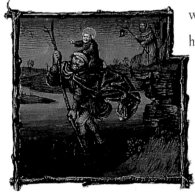

well-known. One stormy night he carried a small child across, struggling and gasping, very nearly collapsing. The child was Christ, who told him he had borne the "weight of the whole world" on his back.

It is a legend and not a history, this story, but it expresses the truth of the saint's name, Christopher, Christ-bearer, to which we are all called and which may sometimes weigh us down with the sorrows of the whole world. Christianity is not an easy option, not an escape. It tackles reality in all its forms, but it does so by the grace of God.

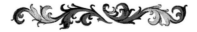

ST GEORGE
Knight of Christ

died c.250

FEAST DAY
April 23rd

PATRON SAINT
*England,
Portugal,
soldiers,
armorers,
archers*

ATTRIBUTES
*dragon,
red cross banner,
princess*

ST GEORGE IS NOT QUITE a legendary saint, because there really was a St. George — an early Christian martyr. He is the knight of Christ, wearing the red cross in his honor, and he lives to rescue the weak and destroy the devil's power. He came across a situation that really needed his help: a whole city weeping. Every year one of their daughters had to be sacrificed to the dragon, and this year the lot had fallen upon the little princess. **T**he artist portrays her delightfully, small and sweet, tucked into the corner of the picture in a glorious blue dress, holding her hands together and praying that her hero will rescue her. What I particularly like about this little picture is the part the horse is playing, because usually the horse is just the vehicle on which St. George rides. Here, I think, the horse is standing for what you might call the "good animal" — our animal powers, our vigor, our enthusiasm. The dragon, of course, is our "bad animal" — our greed, our selfishness, our exploitation of other people. **T**he horse and dragon are confronting one another, eyeball to eyeball. It is only the great spear that St. George thrusts directly down the dragon's gullet that enables the story to end happily. You almost sympathize with the dragon, because he is fighting to the end.

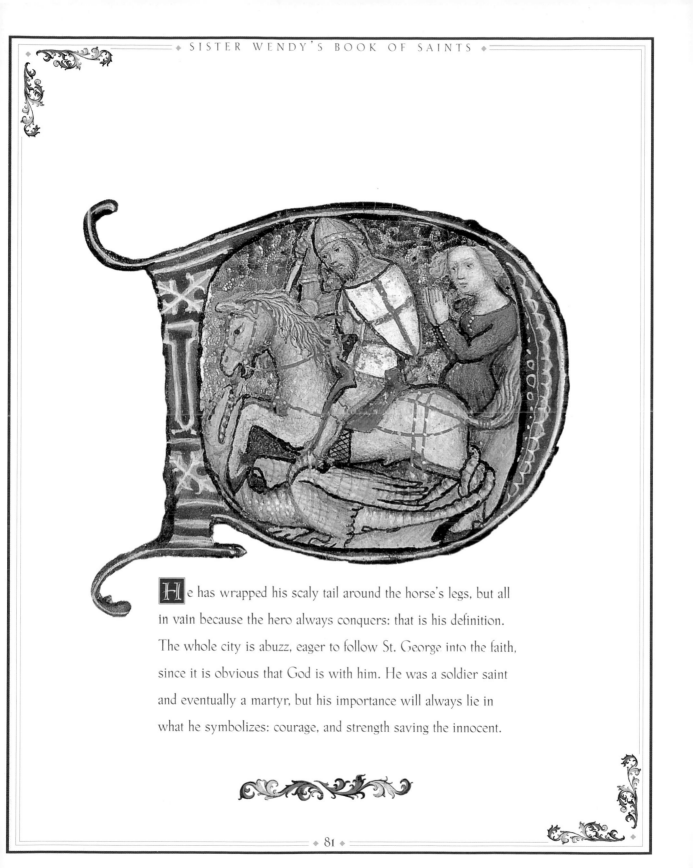

He has wrapped his scaly tail around the horse's legs, but all in vain because the hero always conquers: that is his definition. The whole city is abuzz, eager to follow St. George into the faith, since it is obvious that God is with him. He was a soldier saint and eventually a martyr, but his importance will always lie in what he symbolizes: courage, and strength saving the innocent.

ST MARGARET of ANTIOCH
Virgin martyr

1st Century

FEAST DAY
July 20th

PATRON SAINT
childbirth

ATTRIBUTES
*dragon, crucifix,
pearl rosary*

ST MARGARET WAS A VERY popular saint, because she was the saint to pray to in childbirth, that most dangerous time of a medieval woman's life. Her story may be only a legend, but it is rich in meaning, especially for women. **S**he was said to be sought after in marriage by the Roman governor of Antioch, Olybius, but she wanted no part of him; she was a committed Christian. The painter here shows her innocently turning him down, to general consternation. She had yet to learn, as so many women had yet to learn, that for her there was no freedom to choose. The furious governor thrusts her into prison, where a dark and narrow door

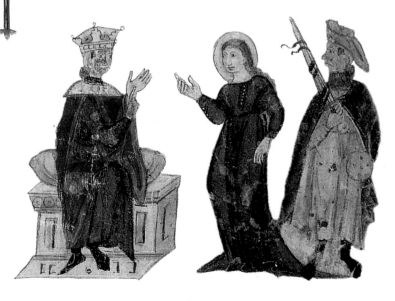

gapes wide: the constrictions of life that she cannot escape.
The prison can never suggest the womb, since the point of
the story is what comes next, the fantasy that she is swallowed
up by a dragon. **T**he fearsome dragon stands for pregnancy
and the inevitability of giving birth. St. Margaret has with her
a small cross, with which she pokes a hole in the dragon and
claws her way out. She comes free from the monster — the
agony of childbirth — into the light of day. **S**he is remarkably
unperturbed, which must have seemed a happy augury for
desperate mothers-to-be. Even if the ordeal ended in
death (as in the last resort did Margaret's, under the
knife), it was still, for one who believed, an escape.

S͏T NICHOLAS
Bishop

4th Century

FEAST DAY
December 6th

PATRON SAINT
*Russia,
children,
pawnbrokers,
sailors,
unmarried girls*

ATTRIBUTES
*three golden
balls or
money bags*

YOU MAY THINK that you do not know anything about the saints, but you know about this one — St. Nicholas. The Dutch shortened Nicholas not to "Nick" but to "Claus," and this is Santa Claus, the great gift-giving saint. He was not a legend but a real person, a bishop who was famous not only for giving but also because he was so sensitive about it. The famous story that sums all this up is the story of the golden balls. St. Nicholas has discovered that there is a nobleman in his diocese who has three daughters and no money. The artist shows him deep in dejection (*see opposite*), because without a

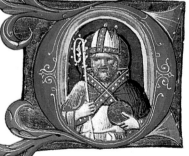

dowry they cannot get married, and there seems nothing for them but a life of prostitution. This greatly distresses Nicholas, who decides he is going to give each one of them a dowry, a golden ball. But he wants no thanks, and he seems to have a pitcher's eye, so he tosses the ball through the window as the daughters sleep.

Here you can see them arriving; he has hit the target with two, and the third golden ball is on its way. The girls are going to wake up to their own personal Christmas morning of glory and relief because they have the one thing they wanted — money for a dowry. That is pure giving because it is secret and alert to the other's needs, not asking any return but to make the other person happy. It is this kind of generosity that makes St. Nicholas a saint. It is tragic that for many people the center of Christmas seems to be a commercial idea of Santa Claus and they forget completely that we are celebrating the birth of Christ, that Jesus and Mary are the meaning of Christmas. But if we know who Santa Claus is, that he is this generous, sweet, sensitive Nicholas who loved to give things to people in need, perhaps we can go through the present-giving and the merrymaking to the true meaning: the birth of Christ.

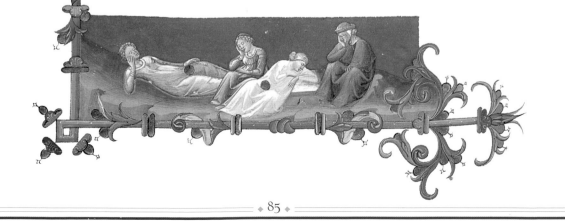

ST. NICHOLAS
Bishop

4th Century

FEAST DAY
December 6th

PATRON SAINT
*Russia,
children,
pawnbrokers,
sailors,
unmarried girls*

ATTRIBUTES
*three golden
balls or
money bags*

ALL THAT WE KNOW for certain about St. Nicholas is that he was a fourth-century bishop of Myra, in southeast Asia, but legends have so swarmed about his name that he is now the most famous of all the saints, under his abbreviated name of "Santa Claus." This little picture shows one of the best-known stories of the saint's amazing miracles. Three little boys disappeared during a famine, while at the same time a rather sinister merchant was advertising

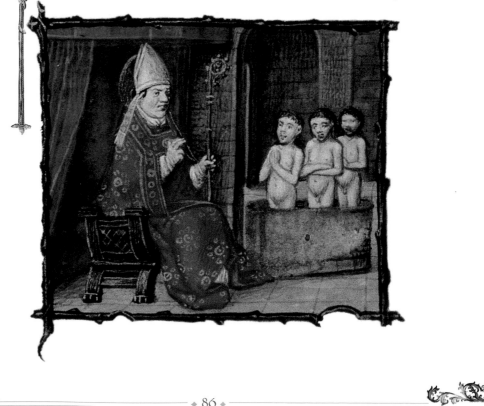

salted pork. St. Nicholas, with a healthy suspicion, asked to
see the barrels, and then blessed them. Out popped the little
boys, naked and alive. What obviously impressed his
contemporaries, and found expression in these stories, was
his power of prayer, his utter certainty that God would always
help him fight for justice. He thought only of his people,
living to help them; and in bringing back to spiritual life those
who had lost their faith, he may well have called those who
were metaphorically pickled in brine back to their youthful
innocence. Here, in the miniature, both saint and children
look equally astonished by God's goodness and power.

ST. GILES
Monk and hermit

died c.710

FEAST DAY
September 1st

PATRON SAINT
*beggers,
cripples,
blacksmiths*

ATTRIBUTES
*wounded stag
or doe*

SAINTS AND ANIMALS are an almost irresistible combination; everybody loves St. Francis because he spoke to the birds and the fish and made friends with the wolf. St. Giles (who, unlike St. Francis, is almost wholly legendary) is famous for his loving devotion to a wild stag. He is said to have become a Benedictine in the end, and an abbot at that, but this touching little miniature shows him in his youth, a hermit living in a cave. A doe's milk kept him alive, and the stag's companionship preserved him from loneliness. Here we see a poignant image of the red-headed saint caressing his four-footed friend. What strikes us is the gentleness, the tender affection, and the animal's trust.

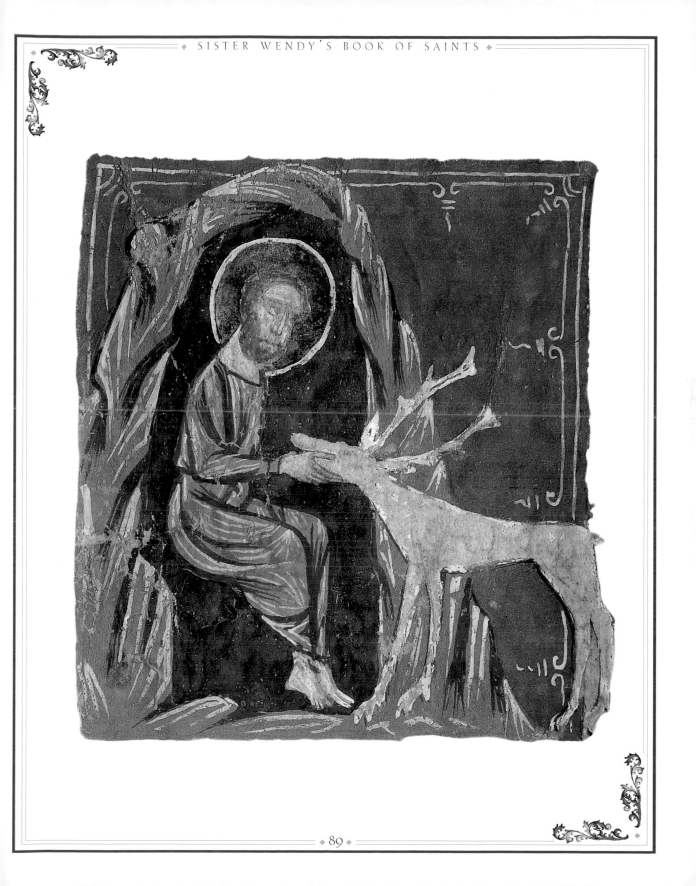

ST. ANNE
Mother of Mary

1st Century BCE

FEAST DAY
July 26th

PATRON SAINT
*Brittany, Canada,
women in labor,
miners*

ATTRIBUTES
*childbirth,
teaching the
Virgin Mary*

SOME OF THE MANUSCRIPTS have miniatures that are extremely small, but the meanings are huge. This little jewel of a picture is all about love, about relationships. We do not really know the name of the Virgin Mary's mother, but the church decided to call her Anne, and here we have her. **S**he is depicted as a comforting figure, a pyramid of the palest pink, with a great gold halo, and nestling

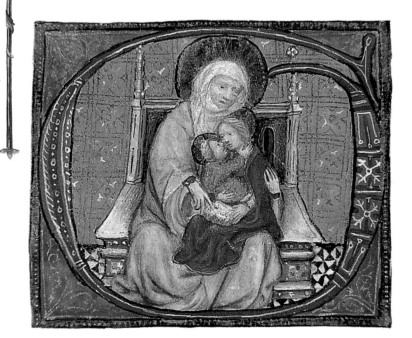

protectively on her mother's lap, in the most heavenly blue, is the Virgin Mary as a little girl. Mary is nursing a tiny golden baby Jesus, who is putting up his little arms to embrace her. Surely, that is what holiness is. You are not a saint because you keep the rules and are blameless; you are a saint if you live in the real world, going out and loving the real people whom God has put into your life. For most of us, this is our own family. So here we have three generations — old Anne, the grandmother, young Mary, the mother, and Jesus, the very small child — and they love and support one another. Because the child is God, it is clear that at the center of all love is God. Or, to put it another way, where love is, God is.

CALENDAR of FEAST DAYS

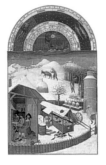

JANUARY

2nd	St. Basil
3rd	St. Geneviève
5th	St. Simeon the Stylite
17th	St. Anthony Abbot
19th	St. Canute
20th	St. Sebastian
21st	St. Agnes
22nd	St. Vincent
26th	St. Paula
28th	St. Thomas Aquinas

FEBRUARY

1st	St. Brigid
3rd	St. Blaise
4th	St. Corsini
5th	St. Agatha
6th	St. Dorothy
9th	St. Apollonia
10th	St. Scholastica
11th	St. Pascal
14th	St. Valentine
15th	St. Sigfrid
24th	St. Ethelbert

MARCH

1st	St. David
3rd	St. Cunegund
4th	St. Casimir
5th	St. Eusebius
10th	St. Anastasia
12th	St. Maximilian
13th	St. Euphrasia
14th	St. Matilda
17th	St. Patrick
18th	St. Frediano
19th	St. Joseph
20th	St. Cuthbert
23rd	St. Gwinear
26th	St. Ludger
31st	St. Acacius

APRIL

7th	St. John-Baptist de la Salle
9th	St. Waudru
12th	St. Zeno of Verona
13th	St. Martin I
16th	St. Bernadette
18th	St. Apollonius
21st	St. Anselm
23rd	St. George
24th	St. Ivo
25th	St. Mark
27th	St. Zita
28th	St. Vitalis
29th	St. Catherine of Siena

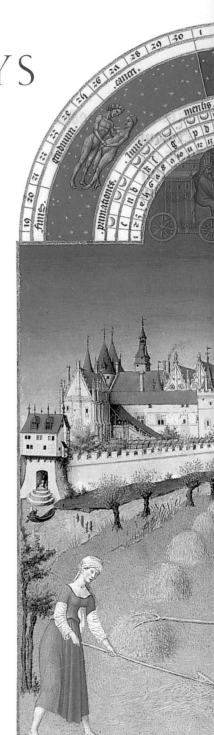

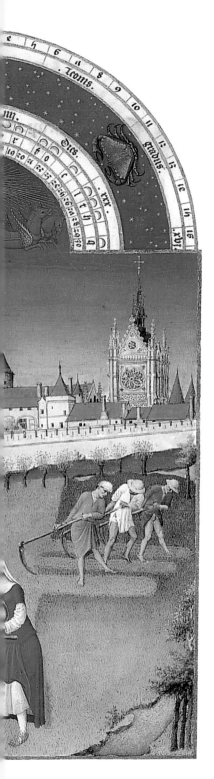

MAY

1st	St. Philip
2nd	St. Athanasius
5th	St. Hilary of Arles
6th	St. Edbert
7th	St. John of Beverley
9th	St. Pachomius
11th	St. Albert of Bergamo
14th	St. Matthias
15th	St. Dympna
16th	St. Brendan
18th	St. Venantius
19th	St. Dunstan
22nd	St. Humility
23rd	St. Desiderius
24th	St. David of Scotland
25th	St. Madeleine Barat
29th	St. Theodosia
30th	St. Joan of Arc
31st	St. Petronilla

JUNE

2nd	St. Erasmus
5th	St. Boniface
6th	St. Norbert
7th	St. Meriadoc
8th	St. William of York
9th	St. Columba
11th	St. Barnabas
13th	St. Antony of Padua
15th	St. Vitus
19th	St. Romuald
21st	St. Aloysius
23rd	St. Ethelreda
24th	St. John the Baptist
27th	St. Cyril of Alexandria
28th	St. Germain of Paris
29th	St. Peter
29th	St. Paul

JULY

1st	St. Simon
3rd	St. Thomas
6th	St. Godelva
11th	St. Benedict
12th	St. Veronica
17th	St. Alexis
20th	St. Margaret of Antioch
22nd	St. Mary Magdalene
23rd	St. Brigit of Sweden
25th	St. Christopher
26th	St. Anne
29th	St. Olaf
31st	St. Ignatius of Loyola

AUGUST

8th	St. Dominic
10th	St. Lawrence
11th	St. Clare
13th	St. Hippolytus
14th	St. Maximilian Kolbe
15th	St. Mary
16th	St. Rock
18th	St. Helena
20th	St. Bernard
24th	St. Bartholomew
27th	St. Monica
28th	St. Augustine of Hippo
30th	St. Fiacre

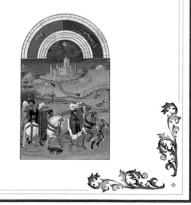

SEPTEMBER

1st	St. Giles
3rd	St. Gregory the Great
4th	St. Rosalia
6th	St. Cagnoald
9th	St. Peter Claver
10th	St. Nicholas Tolentino
13th	St. John Chrysostum
16th	St. Ninian
17th	St. Hildegard
20th	St. Eustace
21st	St. Matthew
23rd	St. Thecla of Iconium
25th	St. Sergius of Radonezh
27th	St. Vincent de Paul
28th	St. Eustochium
28th	St. Wenceslas
29th	St. Michael the Archangel
30th	St. Jerome

OCTOBER

1st	St. Bavo
3rd	St. Teresa of Lisieux
4th	St. Francis of Assisi
6th	St. Bruno
7th	St. Justina
8th	St. Reparata
9th	St. Denis of Paris
11th	St. Bruno the Great of Cologne
12th	St. Wilfrid
13th	St. Edward the Confessor
14th	St. Callistus
15th	St. Teresa of Avila
16th	St. Hedwig
18th	St. Luke
21st	St. Ursula
25th	St. Crispin
28th	St. Jude

NOVEMBER

1st	All Saints' Day
3rd	St. Malachy
7th	St. Engelbert
11th	St. Martin of Tours
12th	St. Joseph of Polotsk
13th	St. Frances Cabrini
22nd	St. Cecilia
23rd	St. Clement I
25th	St. Catherine of Alexandria
30th	St. Andrew

DECEMBER

3rd	St. Francis Xavier
4th	St. Barbara
5th	St. Sabas
6th	St. Nicholas
7th	St. Ambrose
8th	St. Romaric
9th	St. Leocadia
10th	St. Eulalia
13th	St. Lucy
16th	St. Adelaide
21st	St. Thomas
26th	St. Stephen
27th	St. John the Apostle
29th	St. Thomas à Becket

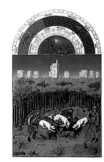

INDEX

ACKNOWLEDGMENTS

PICTURE CREDITS

Abbreviations: ML = Biblioteca Medicea Laurenziana, Florence; Casa = Biblioteca Casanatense,
Rome; Est = Biblioteca Estense e Universitaria, Modena; Mar = Biblioteca Nazionale Marciana,
Venice; Nap = Biblioteca Nazionale "Vittorio Emmanuele III," Naples.

p.1 I B51 c338r Nap; *p.2* Edili 150 c56v ML; *p.3* Ital 1153 clr Est; *p.6* 1898 c3r Casa;
p.7 Mugellano 2 c189r ML; *p.8* Lat I, 77 (=2397) c26v Mar; *p.9* Lat I, 100 (=2098) Mar;
p.11 Corale G206 c2v ML; *p.12* 1909 c277r Casa; *p.15* I B 21 c221r Nap; *p.17* 721 c209v Casa;
p.18 Lat III, 111 (=2116) c134r Mar; *p.19* Lat III, 111 (=2116) c142r Mar; *p.21* Gr. Z. 540 c14v Mar;
p.23 Gr. Z. 540 c215v Mar; *p.25* 721 c223r Casa; *p.27* Lat 74 alpha Q.9. 31 c17r Est;
p.29 1909 c237r Casa; *p.31* XV AA 18 c2v Nap; *p.33* I B51 c326v Nap; *p.34* 1909 c25v Casa;
p.36 I B51 c341v Nap; *p.37* c236r Nap; *p.38* I B51 c338r Nap; *p.41* Corale 2 c46r ML;
p.43 Lat 842 alpha R.7.3 c244r Est; *p.45* Corale 2 c9v ML; *p.47* I B 51 c339v Nap;
p.49 I B51 c330v Nap; *p.51* 1909 c282v Casa; *p.52* Plut. 19.15 c1r ML; *p.53* 620 c149v Casa;
p.54 Conv.Soppr. 304 c109r ML; *p.57* Plut. 12.19 c1 ML; *p.58* 1909 c287v Casa; *p.59* Plut.12.21 c1v ML;
p.61 1909 Casa c246r Casa; *p.63* VII B4 c13r Nap; *p.65* 1182 c295v; *p.66* Med.Palat. 143 c57 ML;
p.67 Ital 1153 clr Est; *p.69* I B51 c322v Nap; *p.71* I B21 c227r Nap; *pp.72–73* Conv.Soppr 457 c 334v ML;
p.75 168 c84r Casa; *p.77* Est 116 c112v Est; *p.78* I B51 c328r Nap; *p.81* 1909 c250r Casa;
p.82 It. Z 13 (=4744) c23r Mar; *p.83* It. Z 13 (=4744) c16v Mar; *pp.84–85* Conv.Soppr. 457 c305v;
p.86 I B51 c324v Nap; *p.89* Est 116 c172v Est; *p.90* 1909 c274r Casa;
pp.92–94 February, June, August, December, from the *Trés Riches Heures du Duc de Berry*,
Musée Condé, Chantilly: Giraudon/Bridgeman Art Library.

AUTHOR'S NOTE
The images in this book have been chosen from a series of exhibitions of
illuminated manuscripts being staged in Italy in 1998–99 to celebrate the Millennium.
Not every saint is represented in these works, so unfortunately some favorite saints,
such as dear St. Patrick, or St. Andrew, for example, could not be included in this selection.